Pilgrimage of the People

Pilgrimage of the People

Liturgies for Labyrinth Worship
throughout the Church Year

Robert J. F. Elsner

WIPF & STOCK · Eugene, Oregon

PILGRIMAGE OF THE PEOPLE
Liturgies for Labyrinth Worship throughout the Church Year

Copyright © 2024 Robert J. F. Elsner. All rights reserved. Except for brief quotations in critical publications or reviews, no part of this book may be reproduced in any manner without prior written permission from the publisher. Write: Permissions, Wipf and Stock Publishers, 199 W. 8th Ave., Suite 3, Eugene, OR 97401.

Wipf and Stock Publishers
199 W. 8th Ave., Suite 3
Eugene, OR 97401

www.wipfandstock.com

PAPERBACK ISBN: 979-8-3852-0497-7
HARDCOVER ISBN: 979-8-3852-0498-4
EBOOK ISBN: 979-8-3852-0499-1

Cataloguing-in-Publication data:

Names: Elsner, Robert J. F. [author].

Title: Pilgrimage of the people : liturgies for labyrinth worship throughout the church year / Robert J. F. Elsner.

Description: Eugene, OR: Wipf and Stock Publishers, 2024 | Includes bibliographical references.

Identifiers: ISBN 979-8-3852-0497-7 (paperback) | ISBN 979-8-3852-0498-4 (hardcover) | ISBN 979-8-3852-0499-1 (ebook)

Subjects: LCSH: Labyrinths. | Labyrinths—Religious aspects—Christianity. | Spiritual life—Christianity. | Prayer—Christianity. | Liturgies.

Classification: BV4509.5 E47 2024 (paperback) | BV4509.5 (ebook)

VERSION NUMBER 03/13/24

Scriptures taken from the KING JAMES VERSION (KJV): KING JAMES VERSION, public domain unless otherwise noted. Scriptures taken from the New Revised Standard Version Bible, copyright 1989, Division of Christian Education of the National Council of the Churches of Christ in the United States of America. Used by permission. All rights reserved. Scriptures marked NIV are taken from THE HOLY BIBLE, NEW INTERNATIONAL VERSION®, NIV® Copyright © 1973, 1978, 1984, 2011 by Biblica, Inc.™ Used by permission. All rights reserved worldwide.

This book is dedicated to
the Glory of God,
and to my beloved wife, Betsy.
We walk with joy in the Lord.

Contents

Acknowledgements | xi

A Note on Using Labyrinths for Liturgies | xiii

Liturgies and Labyrinths | 1

Ordinary Time: Throughout the Church Year
A Liturgy of the Labyrinth | 19

A Church Year of Labyrinth Liturgies
Advent
  Advent 1: Labyrinth Liturgy of Hope | 29
  Advent 2: Labyrinth Liturgy of Peace | 33
  Advent 3: Labyrinth Liturgy of Joy | 36
  Advent 4: Labyrinth Liturgy of Love | 40
  Christmas Eve Labyrinth Liturgy | 46

Christmastide
  Christmas Labyrinth Liturgy | 53
  An Epiphany Liturgy of the Labyrinth | 56

Between Christmastide and Holy Week
  A Liturgy for the Baptism of the Lord | 63
  A Liturgy for the Transfiguration | 67

Contents

A Lenten Liturgy of the Labyrinth | 71

Holy Week and Easter
A Palm Sunday Liturgy of the Labyrinth | 79
An Ash Wednesday Liturgy of the Labyrinth | 82
A Maundy Thursday Liturgy of the Labyrinth | 87
A Good Friday Liturgy of the Labyrinth | 93
A Holy Saturday Liturgy of the Labyrinth | 100

Easter
An Easter Liturgy of the Labyrinth | 107

Between Easter and Trinity Sunday
An Ascension Day Liturgy of the Labyrinth | 113
A Pentecost Liturgy of the Labyrinth | 116
A Trinity Sunday Liturgy of the Labyrinth | 119

Special Labyrinth Liturgies
An All Saints Day Liturgy of the Labyrinth | 125
A Christ the King Sunday Liturgy of the Labyrinth | 129
A Suggested Liturgy for the Washing of Feet | 133

Other Feast Day Liturgies
A Liturgy of the Labyrinth for St. Stephen's Day | 139
A Feast of the Holy Innocents Liturgy of the Labyrinth | 142
A Feast of St. Joseph Liturgy of the Labyrinth | 145
A Feast of Mary Magdalene Liturgy of the Labyrinth | 147
A Feast of St. Mary the Virgin Liturgy of the Labyrinth | 149
A Feast of St. Michael and All Angels Liturgy of the Labyrinth | 152
A Feast of St. James of Jerusalem Liturgy of the Labyrinth | 155

Special Occasion Labyrinth Liturgies
A Liturgy of Healing in the Labyrinth | 161
A Wedding/Anniversary Liturgy in the Labyrinth | 165
A Liturgy of Reconciliation in the Labyrinth | 169
A Labyrinth Liturgy for Liberation | 174

Contents

    A Labyrinth Liturgy for Justice | 177
    A Mother's Day Liturgy for the Labyrinth | 180

Special Public Holiday Liturgies of the Labyrinth
    A Labyrinth Liturgy for Dr. Martin Luther King, Jr. Day | 185
    A Labyrinth Liturgy for Independence Day | 188
    A Labyrinth Liturgy for Columbus/Indigenous People's Day | 191
    A Liturgy of the Labyrinth for Thanksgiving Day | 193
    A Labyrinth Liturgy for President's Day | 196
    A Labyrinth Liturgy for Memorial Day | 199
    A Labyrinth Liturgy for Veteran's Day | 202

Resources and References | 205
About the Author | 207

Acknowledgements

The development of this book and the artwork contained herein was aided by a small grant from the Center for Worship and the Arts at Samford University. My deepest thanks to the staff of the CWA for believing in my vision for this project.

The artwork used between sections of this book are electronic derivatives of a series of paintings and pen-and-ink drawings done by the author during the summer of 2023. All paintings were oil on 4' x 3' canvas, all drawings were pen-and-ink on cartridge paper.

These services are not officially endorsed by any ecclesiastical body and are solely the creation of the author. While they are developed in an Anglican tradition, they borrow from many other Christian traditions. No endorsement or approval is implied from any specific governing body within the church universal.

Special Thanks to Betsy and Sam Elsner for proofreading this manuscript.

A Note on Using Labyrinths for Liturgies

Liturgies are inherently works of people, not individuals, so this book is designed primarily for use by churches or groups of people seeking new worship experiences together to help them focus on their relationships with God and one another. Labyrinths have often been seen as a space for individual contemplation, not corporate worship. There are three major issues to remind you of at this point.

First, not all congregations are blessed with the resources to have their own labyrinth or access to one nearby. Creativity sometimes has to be expressed in defining what a labyrinth is. If there is a room inside like a parish hall, then a labyrinth can be made with tape, toys, or found objects, which can be placed on the floor to create a labyrinth. If an outdoor space is available, using line chalk or line paint can make a great labyrinth for the congregation to try out and the paint or chalk will wear away fairly quickly. If you don't even have such possibilities, map out a course through a public park. Please focus on the benefits of the labyrinth, not the obstacles to doing the practice. Imagination is the basis of a labyrinth and imagination should be nurtured in us all.

Second, congregations are full of people of different ages and abilities. Labyrinths are made to be walked, but not all of us are physically able to walk. For those of us blessed with the ability to walk, walking should be done at one's own pace when alone, or at a mutually comfortable pace with others. For those who cannot

A Note on Using Labyrinths for Liturgies

walk, but are able to use a wheelchair, the same instructions apply. For people unable to journey through the labyrinth with their whole bodies, a cut, carved, or printed copy of a labyrinth can be used. I have created labyrinths by outlining one with dried school glue on paper to help a finger find the way, and another I made by cutting a channel in a block of clay that I then let dry so that I had a labyrinth to journey through.

Third, in this day and age, it is common, even in churches, to abbreviate and expedite services. This is completely oppositional to the liturgies presented here, which are intentionally designed to slow us down and increase contemplation. There are times we should wait and pray. Imagine you are at an altar rail waiting for Communion. If you just rush and get impatient, you have not really received the Body and Blood of our Lord, you had a slightly tasty snack with friends. We are too often like Elijah[1] listening for God in big events. Here, we must slow down in order to listen for the still soft voice of God.

These forms have been written to be led by clergy or laity, so wordings tend to reflect "us" instead of "you" for blessings and other canonically sensitive areas. Changes to the blessings can easily be made by ordained persons to bring them more in line with the liturgical preferences or traditions of the clergy using them.

ORIGINS OF THIS BOOK

I moved to Birmingham, Alabama, in August of 2021, and visited lots of local churches. My family and I decided upon Saint Stephen's Episcopal Church in Vestavia Hills, Alabama, a warm and welcoming parish that is well-known locally as a church that truly reaches out to help others.

At a potluck summer on June 16th of 2022, a gunman opened fire in the parish hall and killed three of our parishioners. Bart, Sharon, and Jane were amazing people who had made me feel welcome when my family and I arrived in Alabama and become a

---

1. 1 Kings 19:11–13

A Note on Using Labyrinths for Liturgies

part of that church. Immediately after the shooting, I was fortunate enough to be there to help provide some comfort and prayer as a psychologist and a theologian. However, I wanted to help further.

During my time serving at a few churches, I was honored to plan and build labyrinths and opened them to communities whose traditions are distant from the High Church one in which I live and move and have my being. Others in the congregation had similar thoughts of constructing a new labyrinth as a memorial to these three martyrs, but we all had a concern of how to incorporate the rest of the congregation into using the labyrinth as a therapeutic and theological focal point.

There is an all-too-common view of labyrinths as an "alternative" individual spiritual tradition. I decided to write a liturgy, as I did not know of any such liturgies for labyrinths, and knew we needed something structured to help people acclimate to using the labyrinth for centering prayer. The first liturgy in this book is that first product. As we used the liturgy, it became clear that we needed more. I found a few prayers and meditations for labyrinth use, but no liturgies in the real sense of structured or semi-structured prayer services that incorporate a labyrinth into actual worship. The following liturgies are for both large and small congregational use.

It is my prayer that these labyrinth liturgies will help people anywhere in the world, even if the people can't walk or roll through them. Prayer finds a way: the way of Jesus.

To God be all glory.

Liturgies and Labyrinths

> Christian worship has never been merely an abstract set of prayers and rubrics which are eternally valid for all times and places, but rather the manner in which people in specific, historical, social, and cultural circumstances express their faith through symbolic ritual. In order to appreciate this necessarily enculturated nature of liturgy it is crucial that we attempt to understand a peoples' way of praying as a whole, as a kind of liturgical system.[1]

In the above quote, Baldovin recognizes that liturgies must change, transform, or be written for the needs of the people. Liturgies are at the core of most Christian worship, even in churches and groups that proclaim themselves to be outside of liturgical traditions. We pray and praise God in myriad ways, sometimes developing new ways over and over again, sometimes using the same formulae and systems as our forbearers used. Liturgies that defy expectations, such as those presented outdoors, have possibilities of teaching the congregation new views and freeing the concept of liturgy from the purely inside form to which most people are accustomed.[2] The earliest liturgies recorded[3] show similarities with what is used to-

---

1. Baldovin, *Liturgy in Ancient Jerusalem*, 3
2. Neville and Westerhoff, *Learning through Liturgy*.
3. In the writings of Bishop Cyril of Jerusalem and the pilgrim Egeria, for example, as cited in Ruth, Steenwyk, and Witvliet, *Walking Where Jesus Walked: Worship in Fourth-Century Jerusalem*.

day in prayers, psalms, and Bible readings from a lectionary, usually interjected with hymns.

At times we do not have historical records, and see through the glass only very darkly, but want to find new light and new ways to glorify God that make sense in our own times. It is to this end that the liturgies in this book have been written. In this work, I have written liturgies to increase a contemplative focus on praising and worshipping God using the sacred spaces of labyrinths. In church history, there are no records I can find of such a thing being written, although that does not mean they did not exist. Liturgies of many faiths share many features, and in Christianity most contain aspects of sacrifice, priesthood, prayer, myth, and ritual,[4] and these components are (hopefully) well represented and obvious in the liturgies contained herein. Liturgies are central to our worship as God's people.

LITURGIES

In liturgy we are always forming and developing our faith. The word liturgy comes from the Greek *leitourgia*, which is a combination of *leitos*, an adjective that means pertaining to the people (*laos*), and *ergon*, a noun which means *work*. To the Greeks, the word meant any service rendered to the public good or the community, even if at personal expense. Developing one's faith is also a work of the people and for the public good as much as it is an action of personal growth and development of faith. Early church liturgies were focused on Scripture, and contained readings of long segments or whole epistles.[5] In Ephesians 5:18b–20, Paul tells us that worshippers should be:

> . . . filled with the Spirit, speaking to one another with psalms, hymns, and songs from the Spirit. Sing and make music from your heart to the Lord, always giving thanks to God the Father for everything, in the name of our Lord Jesus Christ.

4. Price and Weil *Liturgy for Living*.
5. Van Olst, *The Bible and Liturgy*.

Liturgies and Labyrinths

The bedrock of the liturgies of ancient Israel were the Psalms, and the early Christian church built upon these and the Canticles as centers of worship and prayer.[6] Among the most often discussed parts of the Jewish Liturgy is the Mourner's Kaddish, which is a prayer of sanctification:

> Glorified and sanctified be God's great name throughout the world which He has created according to His will.
>
> May He establish His kingdom in your lifetime and during your days, and within the life of the entire House of Israel, speedily and soon; and say, Amen.
>
> May His great name be blessed forever and to all eternity.
>
> Blessed and praised, glorified and exalted, extolled and honored, adored and lauded be the name of the Holy One, blessed be He, beyond all the blessings and hymns, praises and consolations that are ever spoken in the world; and say, Amen.
>
> May there be abundant peace from heaven, and life, for us and for all Israel; and say, Amen.
>
> He who creates peace in His celestial heights, may He create peace for us and for all Israel; and say, Amen.

In the Kaddish, the focus is upon God as the source and inspiration of our prayers, not us. The early Christians, especially the apostles, were still worshiping in the synagogues and the temple, and they were informed by those traditions. There are strong ties to the Lord's Prayer in the structure of Kaddish, and this is central to the liturgies of the church—the focus on God as the source, and the recognition that in even the worst of times we are the beneficiaries of God's grace, mercy, and love. Upon these items is our faith really founded and strengthened.

> Due to its festive nature, for example, liturgy is not ordinary, utilitarian, or for something. Christians do not engage in liturgical worship to get grace or inspiration, to indulge in creativity, to become educated in matters ecclesiastical. Nor do they elaborate rite as a style of life to house nostalgia, to provide rest, to proffer moral

---

6. Van Olst, *The Bible and Liturgy*.

uplift, or to supply aesthetic experience. While any or all of these results may accrue to an individual or an assembly, they constitute neither in whole nor in part the engagement's motive. The feast remains its own end. The business Christians transact in liturgy is festal because, simply, Christ has conquered death by his death. Liturgical theology is therefore a festal endeavor, a doxological rather than any other sort of enterprise. And it is this in a way and to a degree that systematic theology, for all its other virtues, is not.[7]

It is this idea of the festive nature of liturgy that confuses some people. Liturgies do not always seem like feasts, but that is from getting the root word wrong. Feast days are days of joy, where we remember the joy of a life or a miracle. Liturgies are festive, as they are filled with joy, even at a funeral, where the joy is in God's promises and faithfulness.

One of my favorite definitions of liturgy comes from our Catholic sisters and brothers, that "the liturgy is the actualization of the Mystical Body as such," where actualization is the process of formation and development.[8] Liturgy is also the fulfillment of the priestly duties that we are called to do as the priesthood of believers.[9] Some have declared that liturgies should contain sacrifice, priesthood, prayer, myth, and ritual.[10] Sacrifice should be a yielding up of our time and intentions to God, making that which we offer truly holy. Priesthood should be the priesthood of all believers, offering up the sacrifices of a pure and contrite heart in faith and obedience. Prayer should be unceasing, but expressed in ways that help us to learn to pray earnestly and for God's glory, not simply for our needs. Myth is telling the story, even if the events are actual historical events. Rituals are the most visual parts of the liturgies. Ritual is what we are providing here in this book, but instead of raised hands or elevated Host, we see the movement along

---

7. Kavanagh, *On Liturgical Theology*, 151–52.
8. Jacobs, *Orate Fratres*, 506–11.
9. Miller, *Theological Studies*, 325–56.
10. Cf. Price and Weil, *Liturgy for Living*.

the labyrinth and feel the completion of pilgrimage. The rituals of any worship help us as congregations and fellow travelers along the Way of Love that leads us to the Lamb.

LABYRINTHS

Liturgies exist to share in the development of faith. Faith is a journey. At the beginning of the Bible, there are numerous journey motifs. Adam and Eve exiting Eden, Abraham leaving Ur for the promised land, the Children of Israel departing Egypt in the exodus, Jesus walking through the land, and so many more. Journeys are a dominant theme of Scripture. But not all of us have the time or means to go on distant journeys to foreign lands. The labyrinth is *a spiritual journey*, set in a small space and a short time to help people to connect with God and to focus themselves on what is called "contemplative prayer." For too many people, the only time they have heard of a labyrinth is from the famous legend of The Labyrinth and the Minotaur. That labyrinth in Crete was where the intrepid explorer Theseus tracked down and killed the murderous Minotaur.

In the most widely known original story of the labyrinth from Greek mythology, a man named Theseus was led through the labyrinth by a spool of thread given to him by the god Daedalus. The thread allowed him to accomplish his purpose and then find his way out (an oversimplification of the story . . .). He represents every traveler who is guided by a divine instinct through the labyrinth of life and who subjugates the debased, animalistic side of his own nature. While we try to approach these issues differently, the ideals of subduing our internal passions is still an important purpose of journeying through a labyrinth. When we lessen the pull of the animalistic, we achieve union with God in peace, hope, and love. Labyrinths are representations of pilgrimages of some type, although the types and histories differ.

The first recorded Christian pilgrimage was that of a nun named Egeria. She spent several years in the Holy Land, writing to her sisters about the liturgies and practices of worship in the land where Jesus once walked.[11] Egeria's journey occurred somewhere in the late fourth century.[12] Now, not everyone has the financial resources to go to the Holy Land for a few years, but many wanted an experience of getting closer to God through other ways.

It is interesting to note that before Egeria took her pilgrimage, the earliest known Christian labyrinth was a church floor in St. Reparatus Church in El Asnam, Algeria, dating from AD 324, the same year that Constantine began to build St. Peter's in Rome.[13] It comes from a time before pilgrimages were common. In the square, Roman labyrinth of St. Reparatus, four separate five-course sections combine in quadrants to seek the center point, at which a verbal maze includes the words *SANTA ECLESIA* (Holy Church) in several positions on the eight-foot labyrinth.[14] "Holy Church" is an important consideration, as the church should be at the center of our wanderings and musings as we face towards God. The labyrinth, like prayer itself, should be an inward effort (*labor intus*), west to east, from the lands of death to the new life and new light of the rising sun and rising Son.

Labyrinths fell out of favor for fear of being pagan symbols and were not thought about much for hundreds of years. Many of them, like at St. Reparatus, being buried or torn out of churches. By the fourteenth century labyrinths had recovered their positive symbolism and had come to denote the true way of belief.[15] Labyrinths became widely used in gardens and architecture, and beyond famous examples like the floor of Chartres Cathedral, many wonderful examples remain with us around the world. In a strange idiosyncrasy of church history, until the eighteenth century, many cathedrals and churches had labyrinths as ways for people to substitute their walks for great pilgrimages to the Holy

---

11. A translation of her journey can be read at https://www.ccel.org/m/mcclure/etheria/etheria.htm

12. As indicated by references to contemporary materials. See https://www.dbu.edu/mitchell/ancient-christian-resources/egeria.html

13. Wright, *The Maze and the Warrior*.

14. Matthews, *Mazes and Labyrinths*.

15. Fontana, *The Secret Language of Symbols*.

Land. However, they were mostly removed or destroyed during the early eighteenth century, or some, like Chartres, were covered over with wooden floors. Some speculate on the reasons that the labyrinths were removed or covered over, but none of the ideas seem to fit the evidence well.[16]

Labyrinths have been used for numerous religious purposes worldwide. The maze or labyrinth has appeared in the symbolism of ancient Egypt and nearly all early Mediterranean civilizations, and in Indian and Tibetan cultures. Upon the plains of Nasca in Peru, people danced on a flower-shaped labyrinth millennia ago. Most cultures share a symbolic meaning of labyrinths and mazes as expressing ideas of inner journeys through the confusing and conflicting pathways of the mind. The goals are often different, depending on whether the labyrinth was terminal or continuous, but that requires a little bit of explanation and some definitions.

Unfortunately, a maze and a labyrinth are the same thing to the average person. In the Cretan story of the Minotaur, the labyrinth was a maze of doom: a particular type of labyrinth called *multicursal*, as there were numerous courses (which is the circular "layer" of the path that you follow, numbered from the outside to the center) that sometimes dead-ended, and in which travelers could be disoriented and possibly killed by the Minotaur. The multicursal labyrinth is therefore labeled more correctly in common usage as a maze, whereas a more typical labyrinth has a single pathway (which is called *unicursal,* one course) in many courses representing a journey within which the destination is clear. Yale musicologist and historian Craig M. Wright[17] explored the archaeology of mazes and states that in the ancient world, the unicursal labyrinth was an archetype for reality, although the multicursal maze seems to have been the literary and poetic ideal. Music and literature are more interesting if they contain snares and traps, whereas life is better if it doesn't.

While discussing terminology, it is important to point out that in antiquity mazes and labyrinths were the same thing: the

16. Cf. Candolini, *Labyrinths: Walking toward the Center.*
17. Wright, *The Maze and the Warrior.*

difference was whether they were *in bono* (for good) or *in malo* (for harm). The terms "maze" versus "labyrinth" are important to define for their common usage in order to clarify the work of this book. The Oxford English Dictionary defined the following:

> maze / *māz* / noun—a network of paths and hedges designed as a puzzle through which one has to find a way. "the house has a maze and a walled Italian garden."

> lab·y·rinth / ˈlab(ə)ˌrinTH / noun—a complicated irregular network of passages or paths in which it is difficult to find one's way; a maze. "a labyrinth of passages and secret chambers"

Technically, following the OED, there is no difference between these two terms unless we get specific in the modern purposes, such as in spiritual practices. We tend to now use the word labyrinth of *a unicursal maze*, but only in spirituality. That is how we shall use the word in this book. The rest of the world, however, seems to use the two words interchangeably, especially in literature, hundreds of examples of which can be found at most libraries.

To explore the ancient terminology of mazes and labyrinths, what we now distinctly call labyrinths were labeled as *labyrinthos termatikó* in Greek or *labyrinthum termina* in Latin. These labyrinths had a single path (or set of courses) that started at the outside rim, winding inward, and ended in the center. A *labyrinthum iugis* or *labyrinthum contunua*[18] does not end in the center, but rather uses the center point as a position of worship or discovery from which the traveler must continue the symbolic journey, as if bringing the newfound treasure—usually peace or knowledge—back to the world by a slightly different route. These continuous labyrinths are therefore more theologically appropriate to Christian theology, as we are changed after any encounter with God and our paths continue, hopefully bringing the gospel back to the world.

Labyrinths and mazes are often described by their overall shape (round, square, rectangular, octagonal, etc.) and number of

---

18. the Greek term *labyrinthum synechízontas* is almost never used

courses (folded paths counted from the center to the edge). The labyrinth at Chartres is a round twelve-course labyrinth, and also features, like many others in churches, a *sacred geometry*, as it balances a sacred number of courses between the four cardinal points as on a cross.

Figure 1. Example plan of a *labyrinthum iugis* or *labyrinthum contunua* (continuous labyrinth).

CONTEMPLATIVE PRAYER

Using the modern definitions, mazes, as opposed to labyrinths, are not typically considered appropriate for centering, meditative prayer. This is because prayer within or without a maze would be about finding one's way out of difficulty, not risking getting trapped inside and killed by mythical beasts. Walking a labyrinth, by contrast, is a way of helping a person to center her or his prayers on God. This thought might sound strange, but many people do not know how to pray, or are kinesthetic learners who need to be doing something to help them to focus on God instead of being distracted away from God. I have had many parishioners with OCD, ADHD, or who are on the autistic spectrum for whom the labyrinth was an amazing revelation about worship that allowed them to express themselves before God in the fullness of their being.

In the classic work on centering prayer, M. Basil Pennington[19] refers to the words of Paul in 1 Corinthians 2:1–16.[20] They are worth reproducing here in its entirety:

> And I, brethren, when I came to you, came not with excellency of speech or of wisdom, declaring unto you the testimony of God. For I determined not to know any thing among you, save Jesus Christ, and him crucified. And I was with you in weakness, and in fear, and in much trembling. And my speech and my preaching was not with enticing words of man's wisdom, but in demonstration of the Spirit and of power: That your faith should not stand in the wisdom of men, but in the power of God.
>
> Howbeit we speak wisdom among them that are perfect: yet not the wisdom of this world, nor of the princes of this world, that come to nought: But we speak the wisdom of God in a mystery, even the hidden wisdom, which God ordained before the world unto our glory: Which none of the princes of this world knew: for had they known it, they would not have crucified the Lord of glory.
>
> But as it is written, Eye hath not seen, nor ear heard, neither have entered into the heart of man, the things which God hath prepared for them that love him.
>
> But God hath revealed them unto us by his Spirit: for the Spirit searcheth all things, yea, the deep things of

---

19. Pennington, *Centering Prayer*.

20. All translations are either from the KJV or NIV (unless specified otherwise).

> God. For what man knoweth the things of a man, save the spirit of man which is in him? even so the things of God knoweth no man, but the Spirit of God. Now we have received, not the spirit of the world, but the Spirit which is of God; that we might know the things that are freely given to us of God. Which things also we speak, not in the words which man's wisdom teacheth, but which the Holy Ghost teacheth; comparing spiritual things with spiritual.
>
> But the natural man receiveth not the things of the Spirit of God: for they are foolishness unto him: neither can he know them, because they are spiritually discerned. But he that is spiritual judgeth all things, yet he himself is judged of no man. For who hath known the mind of the Lord, that he may instruct him? But we have the mind of Christ.

Like Paul, most of us do not come to prayer in excellency of words or understanding, but in hope and faith. Often our understanding of faith is more akin to the father of the sick child in Mark 9:23–24:

> Jesus said unto him, If thou canst believe, all things are possible to him that believeth. And straightway the father of the child cried out, and said with tears, Lord, I believe; help thou mine unbelief.

It is because of our unbelief that we need to pray and to focus our prayers on God, centering ourselves to seek God more fully. Too often, alas, the idea of centering prayer is not focused on God, and not even on the self, but on a method or way of centering that becomes the object of the center itself.[21] Teresa of Avila taught that when we pray, especially without understanding of great words, we should consider ourselves as a castle, with God dwelling at the center of the soul, and desirous of us coming back to that center.[22]

Thomas Keating, a monk who is given a lot of the credit for reviving the Christian tradition of walking the labyrinth, focused

---

21. Pennington, *Finding Grace at the Center.*
22. Kavanaugh, "Contemplation and the Stream of Consciousness."

on the idea of centering prayer as a form of contemplation. He says that the word "contemplation" used to mean different things. When you think of it, you probably see it as being an intention of a future act. In the 1590s, it meant reflecting on, studying, or meditating. In the early church it meant observation (*con-* means *with*; *templum* means an area for taking auguries, not just a place of worship).[23]

In the early church, contemplative prayer was seen as a worthy thing, whereas from the sixth century on, Keating tells us that most people thought contemplative prayer to be indulgent. We know that recitation of Scripture was seen as more important in many ways, especially following Erasmus's call that "I would to God that the plowman would sing a text of the Scripture at his plow and that the weaver would hum them to the tune of his shuttle."[24] Prayer was often considered to be essential for life, but only for focused purposes of worship and request. Keating says[25] that we should be praying for wisdom and an ever-increasing intimacy with God as *abba* (an Aramaic word even more intimate than our word *father*). The problem is often that so many earthly fathers are not great examples of what a father should be, so people react against this term, comparing our heavenly and perfect Father with our fallen and human fathers. Recognizing this essential issue helps us to be sympathetic to some who are averse to gender-specific terms for God, due to the trauma of bad parenting.

What Keating was talking about can be translated from the Rule of Saint Benedict as: "Listen with the ear of your heart."[26] If we are to listen to God while praying, not just telling God what we want or think we need, then we need to be in a spiritual and psychological condition to hear what God might be telling us. As the old adage goes, no prayer goes unanswered, but sometimes the answer is "no."

---

23. https://www.etymonline.com/word/contemplate
24. Wallraff, Menchi, and Greyerz, *Basel 1516*.
25. Keating, *Finding Grace at the Center*.
26. Rule of Benedict, prologue 1.

In his lovely book on contemplative prayer, Danaher gives us an excellent guide to the levels of prayer and knowing:

> [T]he Carthusian, a twelfth-century monk, claimed that there were three levels of prayer. The first is all about words and mostly our petitioning of God for things we desire. There is nothing wrong with that, but it does not take us very far on the spiritual journey. The second level is that of meditation. This form of prayer is largely a matter of meditating on a Scripture. Often referred to as *Lectio Divina*, it is more about ideas than words. The third level of contemplative prayer and it is about neither words nor ideas but instead is simply a matter of being aware of God's presence and resting in that presence.
>
> As there are levels of prayer, there are likewise levels of knowing. We may know certain facts about a person but that does not mean that we know that person. In order to know someone, we must spend time with that person. Think of the celebrities you "know" a lot about but whom you do not know because you have never spent time with them. The same is true of God. Many people "know" and believe certain facts about God, but it is only as we spend time in his presence that we come to know him. Furthermore, the best way to spend time in God's presence is in silence in order that God might commune with us beyond words as lovers often do with a silent gaze. His is the mystery of contemplative prayer.[27]

The idea here is that if we know God, just as if we know one another, we can more truly and fully love God and each other. Each step we take in knowing and understanding brings a closeness and trust that is strong.

If one were to ask "How does a labyrinth help our church?," there are several answers one could give:[28] improving mission, sharing worship, building community, and growing in wisdom are some of the things that labyrinths provide through their appropriate use in contemplation and focus of prayer. A problem that has

---

27. Danaher, *Contemplative Prayer*, xiii
28. Welch, *Walking the Labyrinth*.

often occurred in church labyrinths usage, however, is that there are *no established liturgies for communal use*. The labyrinth is seen as an indulgence and as only for personal use, so it can separate the congregations that it is supposed to bind together. Martin says that there is a two-beat rhythm of revelation and response that makes up the distinctive genius of corporate worship.[29] When we worship, we should be seeking both the revelation of Scripture and the responses both *to* God and *from* God. This interchange needs to be set in a rhythm to help us establish our worship habits and learn from each other and from ourselves. This is why we have and need liturgies—a liberative teaching tool to help us get to know God in an orthodox and listening manner.

For many years I have taught new counselors that there are two ways of listening. The first way is to *reflect focus*: to get enough information from someone to reflect the focus of the conversation on ourselves. If your friend says "I had such a hard day . . ." and you respond with "You think *YOU* had a hard day? Well, listen to what *MY* day was . . . ." This shows no sympathy or empathy for your friend, but a strong desire to be listened to and cared for. We should not be doing this to God, only begging for what we want and need. The second way of listening is to *understand*. When your friend has a hard day, do you ask for more information so that you can know and feel for that person? What about with God? If God says "THOU SHALL" or "THOU SHALL NOT," we tend to not ask many questions unless we are trying to get around those commandments. What if we listen in order to understand and then to really get to know God? This is the basis for worship and the best of prayer.

Like prayer, however, labyrinths are best accomplished if we prepare ourselves beforehand, and consider what we have done afterwards, listening for that small, soft voice of God within ourselves. In a lovely book on contemplative prayer, Paintner and Wynkoop remind us that preparing for truly listening for God's word involves several steps.[30] First, we must be reading God's word

---

29. Martin, *The Worship of God*.
30. Paintner & Wynkoop, *Lectio Divina*.

(*lectio*), reflecting on God's word (*meditatio*), responding to God's word (*oratio*), resting with God's word (*contemplatio*), and becoming God's word (*operatio*). This is a set of operations that come into play with the labyrinth. Read and pray before walking, but make sure to continue this work while walking and afterwards. Through this, we truly can start to listen to understand God carefully.

Christian labyrinths should always be a reminder of the hope in God's promise to us—that God wants us to repent of our sins, but also to worship directly in a personal relationship of love and respect. One of the least-often cited parts of Scripture that points to this level of love, respect, and hope is from Hosea 2:14–16, 19–20

> [14]Therefore, I will now allure her,
>   and bring her into the wilderness,
>   and speak tenderly to her.
> [15]From there I will give her her vineyards,
>   and make the Valley of Achor a door of hope.
> There she shall respond as in the days of her youth,
>   as at the time when she came out of the land of Egypt.
> [16]On that day, says the LORD, you will call me, "My husband," and no longer will you call me, "My Baal."
> [17]For I will remove the names of the Baals from her mouth, and they shall be mentioned by name no more.
> [18]I will make for you a covenant on that day with the wild animals, the birds of the air, and the creeping things of the ground; and I will abolish the bow, the sword, and war from the land; and I will make you lie down in safety.
> [19]And I will take you for my wife forever; I will take you for my wife in righteousness and in justice, in steadfast love, and in mercy. [20]I will take you for my wife in faithfulness; and you shall know the LORD.

Our relationship must change, and our closeness to God must remove us from our closeness to the world from which we came. In verse 16 above, most of us read the word "Baal" and think of a false god of the Canaanites. However, "Baal" here is used to indicate "Lord" or "Master" in a more mundane sense of social hierarchy. This use of "Baal" indicates difference and separation of the "other" instead of the close, loving, and personal relationship that God wants with us. This continues in the next verse, where the names of the Baals are the names of other masters or lords who held sway over Israel. These statements indicate a change in relationship of love and devotion that is two way, like in a marriage—instead of "Master," one becomes "Beloved." The centering on God as Father in a pure, holy way will occasionally be uncomfortable, just as walking a labyrinth is sometimes uncomfortable or discomforting.

For many of us, the theology of the labyrinths are to be understood as one of two things. First, with a *labyrinthos termatikó/ labyrinthum termina* like the very famous one at Chartres, we journey with Christ to Jerusalem as the center, pray, and then return the exact way we came, or we simply walk off the labyrinth any way we like (because there are too many tourists on it at Chartres to walk back the way we came). This is less desirous theologically, as it either tells us to depart following any movement, not necessarily that of the Spirit, or to retrace our footsteps and end in the same place we began, which is far from the examples of disciples and saints. A *labyrinthum iugis* or *labyrinthum contunua* is closer to the Christian ideal in many ways, as we never end up where we started, having been changed by the power of the Holy Spirit.

After the resurrection, none of the disciples simply went home and carried on their lives as they were, nor should we after an encounter with God in a labyrinth. As Marshall McLuhan is famous for saying, "the medium is the message."[31] How we frame things and how we present them are the driving forces behind the *take-away* that people get. If we put forward a labyrinth that leaves ambiguity in its completion, we leave ambiguity as to the final message of the labyrinth and the centering on God that applies in our lives. While this idea may not be well received by some, it is a careful reflection on theological studies that is eminently defensible. Progress is made as Scripture is read and studied.

---

31. McLuhan, *Understanding Media*.

Ordinary Time:
Throughout the Church Year

Liturgy literally means "work of the people," but can also be understood to be the work of a person in place of a group of people. Just as at times many a layperson, deacon, or priest has said Morning Prayer or Evening Prayer by themselves for the congregation, it is completely acceptable to walk the labyrinth for the rest of the church. These liturgies can be read by a single person saying all parts, or by several people or large groups. The important part is that you pray to prepare, pray to walk, and pray to transition to your work in the world.

If weather prohibits the use of an outdoor labyrinth, a canvas or cloth one could be used if available. If not, one can be marked of in tape on a floor, or even be outlined by toys, rocks, candles, chalk, etc. Don't let the lack of access to a physical outdoor labyrinth stop the use of these walks. Remember that they are developed to help focus on the "reason for the season."

Figure 2. Communion at IPC, Birmingham, inspired by da Vinci. © Rob Elsner

A Liturgy of the Labyrinth

A general service using the labyrinth as a location for worship.[1] *This service is appropriate for any time of the church year, but most especially for that called "Ordinary Time" except when there is a special feast day. If desired and possible in the space, the color green is preferred for decorations, banners, ribbons, etc.*

THE OPENING

The congregation gathers by the labyrinth and stands or sits in prayer and quiet contemplation.

Reader: A voice cries out: "In the wilderness prepare the way of the LORD, make straight in the desert a highway for our God. Every valley shall be lifted up, and every mountain and hill be made low; the uneven ground shall become level, and the rough places a plain. Then the glory of the LORD shall be revealed, and all people shall see it together, for the mouth of the LORD has spoken." *(Isaiah 40:3-4)*

---

1. This can be seen as an *Ordinary Time* liturgy. A green frontal and green should be used for any hangings or decorations associated with the labyrinth space, if such exist in your location.

Ordinary Time: Throughout the Church Year

Leader: If we say that we have no sin, we deceive ourselves, and the truth is not in us; but if we confess our sins, God is faithful and just to forgive us our sins, and to cleanse us from all unrighteousness. *(1 John 1:8, 9)*

Sisters and Brothers in Christ, we gather in praise of God through our words and our silence, through movements, and through the opening of our hearts to God's loving faithfulness. We travel through this labyrinth in faithfulness of heart, seeking God's peace and mercy.

(Please consider using the asterisks below/above for pauses or indicators of change if responsively reading by half verse.)

Together: O be joyful in the Lord all ye lands; *
    serve the Lord with gladness
    and come before his presence with a song.
Be ye sure that the Lord he is God;
it is he that hath made us and not we ourselves; *
    we are his people and the sheep of his pasture.
O go your way into his gates with thanksgiving
and into his courts with praise; *
    be thankful unto him and speak good of his Name.
For the Lord is gracious;
his mercy is everlasting; *
    and his truth endureth from generation to generation. *(Jubilate. Psalm 100)*
Glory to the Father, and the Son, and to the Holy Spirit:*
    as it was in the beginning, is now, and will be forever. Amen.

Leader: The Lord be with you.
People: And also with you.
Leader: Let us pray.

Together: Our Father, who art in heaven,

A Liturgy of the Labrinth

>   hallowed be thy Name,
>   thy kingdom come,
>   thy will be done,
>   on earth as it is in heaven.
> Give us this day our daily bread.
> And forgive us our trespasses,
>   as we forgive those who trespass against us.
> And lead us not into temptation,
>   but deliver us from evil.
> For thine is the kingdom, and the power, and the glory,
>   for ever and ever. Amen.

Leader: O Lord, show your mercy upon us;
People: And grant us your salvation.
Leader: Endue your ministers with righteousness;
People: And make your chosen people joyful.
Leader: Give peace, O Lord, in all the world;
People: For only in you can we live in safety.
Leader: Lord, keep this nation under you care;
People: And guide us in the way of justice and truth.
Leader: Let your way be known upon earth;
People: Your saving health among all nations.
Leader: Let not the needy, O Lord, be forgotten;
People: Nor the hope of the poor be taken away.
Leader: Heal those of us broken in mind and body;
People: That we may be your hands and feet.
Leader: Strengthen our spirit and faith;
People: Our hope of eternity in you.
Leader: Let each turn in this labyrinth guide us to you;
People: And release us from sin, oppression, and stress.
Leader: Create in us clean hearts, O God;
People: And sustain us with your Holy Spirit.

For optional use, when desired, and if suitable for the weather conditions of an outdoor labyrinth, a basin of holy water should be made available. A foot washing is appropriate, possibly using the suggested

Ordinary Time: Throughout the Church Year

form on pp. 132–34, or the following, each person dipping fingers into the water, then touching the appropriate parts:

> Bless, O Lord, these hands, that they may provide care and protection;
> Bless, O Lord, these eyes, that they may only see truth;
> Bless, O Lord, these ears, that they may hear love;
> Bless, O Lord, this mouth, that words of your glory are spoken;
> Bless, O Lord, these feet, that they may walk in your way and follow you always.

Leader: Almighty God, to you all hearts are open, all desires known, and from you no secrets are hid: Cleanse the thoughts of our hearts by the inspiration of your Holy Spirit, that we may perfectly love you, and worthily magnify your holy Name. You set the foundations of the earth and the boundaries of the sea, now guide our feet, our hearts, and our minds to love and serve you always. Let each footfall or movement forward be a new connection to you and your love, Creator, Redeemer, and Friend. Give us strength and grace with each course of this labyrinth, that walking or wheeling we dance in praise of you; that with joy we hear the angelic rhythm unseen or unheard except in the hearts of believers; through Christ our Lord. *Amen.*

THE LABYRINTH

The people now begin the labyrinth in whatever way is most practical for the space. When each person has completed the journey, they should stand or be seated in silent prayer until all are finished. The labyrinth courses may be followed in silence or in singing of a chant, such as "Ubi Caritas" as appropriate to the traditions of the congregation.

A Liturgy of the Labyrinth

OPTIONAL COMMUNION

Here may be added a celebration of the Holy Eucharist or add special prayers:

THE PROCESSION INTO THE WORLD

Leader: Let us pray.

Together: Almighty and everliving God, we most heartily thank you for the centering of our hearts and minds on you, your mercy, and your love for us. We beg your mercy that our path may be simple and wide, with no stumbling blocks before us. Heal our brokenness where we are afflicted in mind, body, or spirit. Strengthen us for service, O God, that we may share with others the peace and calm you have given to us. Have mercy on us, beloved Lord, through Jesus Christ, to whom, with you and the Holy Ghost, be all honor and glory, world without end. *Amen.*

Leader: The peace of God, which passes all understanding, keep our hearts and minds in the knowledge and love of God, and mercy and compassion of Jesus Christ, and the guidance and fellowship of the Holy Spirit. The blessing of God Almighty, the Father, the Son, and the Holy Ghost, be amongst us, and remain with us always. *Amen.*

Leader: Go in peace to love and serve the Lord.
People: Thanks be to God.

A Church Year of
Labyrinth Liturgies

Figure 3. Nativity at the Amiens Labyrinth,
inspired by Lorenzo Lotto © Rob Elsner

Advent

Advent is a time in which we anticipate the coming of Jesus and renew our faith and love of God. Advent literally means "to come." It is a time of anticipation and renewal. As a season, Advent is four-weeks long, beginning with the fourth Sunday before Christmas and continuing through Christmas Eve. Advent is the beginning of the church year, and sets the mood for the entire year as one of hope, peace, joy, and love.

Each of the four weeks are represented by the candles of the Advent wreath. The first week centers on *hope* and is illuminated by the Prophecy Candle (purple). Week 2 is focused on *peace*, lit by the Bethlehem Candle (also purple). The third week, *joy*, is represented by the pink candle, called the Shepherd's Candle. The final week is about *love*, with the Angel Candle (purple) completing the wreath.

Advent 1: Labyrinth Liturgy of Hope

If desired and possible in the space, the colors violet or royal blue are preferred for decorations, banners, ribbons, etc.

THE OPENING

The congregation gathers by the labyrinth and stands or sits in prayer and quiet contemplation.

Leader: May the God of hope fill you with all joy and peace in believing, so that by the power of the Holy Spirit you may abound in hope. *(Romans 15:13)*

People: Now faith is the assurance of things hoped for, the conviction of things not seen. *(Hebrews 11:1)*

Leader: For in this hope we were saved. Now hope that is seen is not hope. For who hopes for what he sees? But if we hope for what we do not see, we wait for it with patience. *(Romans 8:24–25)*

Leader: Beloved in Christ, we gather to focus our minds, our hearts, and our lives on the hope of this Advent season. Why, my soul, are you downcast?

Advent

> Why so disturbed within me?
> Put your hope in God,
> for I will yet praise him,
> my Savior and my God. (*Psalm 42:11*)

People: But those who hope in the Lord
will renew their strength.
They will soar on wings like eagles;
they will run and not grow weary,
they will walk and not be faint. (*Isaiah 40:31*)

Leader The Lord be with you.
People And also with you.
Leader: Let us pray.

Together: Our Father, who art in heaven,
    hallowed be thy Name,
    thy kingdom come,
    thy will be done,
        on earth as it is in heaven.
Give us this day our daily bread.
And forgive us our trespasses,
    as we forgive those who trespass against us.
And lead us not into temptation,
    but deliver us from evil.
For thine is the kingdom, and the power, and the glory,
    for ever and ever. Amen.

Leader: Sisters and Brothers in Christ, we gather in praise of God through our words and our silence, through movements, and through the opening of our hearts to God's loving faithfulness. We travel through this labyrinth in faithfulness of heart, seeking God's peace and mercy. Let us remember those who hoped for Jesus' birth and sought him out. They came from afar and were led by a star. Let the bright shining hope of Christ lead us through the twists and turns of this labyrinth.

Advent 1: Labyrinth Liturgy of Hope

THE LABYRINTH

The people now begin the labyrinth in whatever way is most practical for the space. When each person has completed the journey, they should stand or be seated in silent prayer until all are finished. The labyrinth courses may be followed in silence or in singing of a chant, such as "The Light of Christ! Alleluia!" or rounds of "Seek Ye First the Kingdom of God" as appropriate to the traditions of the congregation.

OPTIONAL COMMUNION

Here may be added a celebration of the Holy Eucharist or the following:

Leader: Creator, sustainer, redeemer of all, who has inspired minds and hearts through all ages to seek you. We praise you and thank you for the ability to follow the wise who have travelled afar seeking you. Inspire in our hearts the drive to continually seek you. Even when we cannot traverse the ground, empower us to follow wherever you lead, praising you and loving you now and always. *Amen.*

THE PROCESSION INTO THE WORLD

Leader: Let us pray.

Together: Spirit of love and peace, who came to earth for our salvation, lead us on to your love. Show our hearts and minds the promise of the true hope that binds us to you and to each other. Give us further hope to see your kingdom on earth as beautiful, just, and merciful as your kingdom in heaven. Tie us together with unbreakable cords of hope that we may build this kingdom for you and with you. *Amen.*

Advent

Leader: The Lord of Hope, who led the shepherds, angels, and kings to Bethlehem to worship at your birth, bless us and keep us. May the Spirit of Love overwhelm us with joy today and forever. And the blessing of God Almighty, the Father, the Son, and the Holy Ghost, be amongst us, and remain with us always. *Amen.*

Leader: Go in peace and hope to love and serve the hope of all nations.
People Thanks be to God.

Advent 2:
Labyrinth Liturgy of Peace

If desired and possible in the space, the colors violet or royal blue are preferred for decorations, banners, ribbons, etc.

THE OPENING

Leader: But the Advocate, the Holy Spirit, whom the Father will send in my name, will teach you all things and will remind you of everything I have said to you. ²eace I leave with you; my peace I give you. I do not give to you as the world gives. Do not let your hearts be troubled and do not be afraid. You heard me say, "I am going away and I am coming back to you." If you loved me, you would be glad that I am going to the Father, for the Father is greater than I. (*John 14:26–28*)

People: Give us your peace, O God, and hear us when we call to you.

Leader: We are troubled and fight one another in ways we do not always know.

People: Give us your peace, O God, and hear us when we call to you.

Advent

Leader:	We cause pain in ourselves and in others because we lack faith in you and your promises.
People:	Give us your peace, O God, and hear us when we call to you.
Leader:	Send us angels of peace, beloved Lord, that we can overcome our fear and be glad for one another.
People:	Give us your peace, O God, and hear us when we call to you.
Leader:	Help us to return to you, Holy One, and let our hearts no longer be troubled.
People:	Give us your peace, O God, and hear us when we call to you.
All:	Let us not be afraid, but trust in your peace.

THE LABYRINTH

The people now begin the labyrinth in whatever way is most practical for the space. When each person has completed the journey, they should stand or be seated in silent prayer until all are finished. The labyrinth courses may be followed in silence or in repeating the word "Peace" or phrase "Give us your peace" while walking.

OPTIONAL COMMUNION

Here may be added a celebration of the Holy Eucharist or the following:

Leader: "Come unto me, all ye that labour and are heavy laden, and I will give you rest. Take my yoke upon you, and learn of me; for I am meek and lowly in heart: and ye shall find rest unto your souls. For my yoke is easy, and my burden is light" *(Matthew 11:28-30).* O God of Peace, lover of concord, who sent your Son to be the Prince of Peace, plant faith and true peace in our hearts that we may abandon fear and doubt. Let all wars and divisions cease. Take away the hatred and jealousy that destroy the unity of your people.

People: "Listen! Do not fear. For I bring you good news of great joy, which will be to all people. For unto you is born this day in the City of David a Savior, who is Christ the Lord. And this will be a sign to you: You will find the Baby wrapped in strips of cloth, lying in a manger." Suddenly there was with the angel a company of the heavenly host praising God and saying, "Glory to God in the highest, and on earth peace, and good will toward men." *Amen. (Luke 2)*

THE PROCESSION INTO THE WORLD

Together: We await your coming, O Christ. We yearn for your peace. Peace you give us, let us learn to see it and partake of it. Let us see your truth and have courage to stand up to all that steals our peace. Set yourself as a seal upon our hearts, O God, that jealousy and evil cannot enter, and peace can grow. *Amen.*

Leader: Peace I leave with you, my peace I give unto you: not as the world giveth, give I unto you. Let not your heart be troubled, neither let it be afraid. *(John 14:27)* The Lord of Peace, who sent angels with messages of peace, enfold us in tranquility and happiness. And the blessing of God Almighty, the Father, the Son, and the Holy Ghost, be amongst us, and remain with us always. *Amen.*

Leader: Let us go in peace to love and serve the fount of all peace.
People: Thanks be to God.

Advent 3:
Labyrinth Liturgy of Joy

If desired and possible in the space, the colors violet or royal blue are preferred for decorations, banners, ribbons, etc. For the third Sunday, also known as Gaudete Sunday,[1] pink may be considered appropriate.

THE OPENING

Leader: And, lo, the angel of the Lord came upon them, and the glory of the Lord shone round about them: and they were sore afraid. And the angel said unto them, Fear not: for, behold, I bring you good tidings of great joy, which shall be to all people. For unto you is born this day in the city of David a Saviour, which is Christ the Lord. (*Luke 2:9–11*)

When they had heard the king, they departed; and, lo, the star, which they saw in the east, went before them, till it came and stood over where the young child was. When they saw the star, they rejoiced with exceeding great joy. And when they were come into the house,

---

1. Gaudete is the Latin word for "Rejoice," which was the first word appearing in the old pre-Reformation liturgies for that day.

Advent 3: Labyrinth Liturgy of Joy

they saw the young child with Mary his mother, and fell down, and worshipped him: and when they had opened their treasures, they presented unto him gifts; gold, and frankincense and myrrh. (*Matthew 2:9–11*)

PRAYERS OF THE PEOPLE

Leader: Let them shout for joy, and be glad, that favour my righteous cause: yea, let them say continually, Let the Lord be magnified, which hath pleasure in the prosperity of his servant. (*Psalm 35:27*)

People: But let all those that put their trust in thee rejoice: let them ever shout for joy, because thou defendest them: let them also that love thy name be joyful in thee. (*Psalm 5:11*)

Leader: For his anger endureth but a moment; in his favour is life: weeping may endure for a night, but joy cometh in the morning. (*Psalm 30:5*)

People: Let the saints be joyful in glory: let them sing aloud upon their beds. (*Psalm 149:5*)

Leader: He maketh the barren woman to keep house, and to be a joyful mother of children. Praise ye the Lord. (*Psalm 113:9*)

People: Make me to hear joy and gladness; that the bones which thou hast broken may rejoice. (*Psalm 51:8*)

Leader: Go your way, eat the fat, and drink the sweet, and send portions unto them for whom nothing is prepared: for this day is holy unto our Lord: neither be ye sorry; for the joy of the Lord is your strength. (*Nehemiah 8:10*)

People: And I will rejoice in Jerusalem, and joy in my people: and the voice of weeping shall be no more heard in her, nor the voice of crying. (*Isaiah 65:19*)

Leader: Then shall the virgin rejoice in the dance, both young men and old together: for I will turn their mourning into joy, and will comfort them, and make them rejoice from their sorrow. (*Jeremiah 31:13*)

Advent

People: Yet I will rejoice in the Lord, I will joy in the God of my salvation. *(Habakkuk 3:18)*

Leader: And David spake to the chief of the Levites to appoint their brethren to be the singers with instruments of musick, psalteries and harps and cymbals, sounding, by lifting up the voice with joy. *(1 Chronicles 15:16)*

People: But the fruit of the Spirit is love, joy, peace, longsuffering, gentleness, goodness, faith, meekness, temperance: against such there is no law. *(Galatians 5:22–23)*

Leader: Blessed are ye, when men shall hate you, and when they shall separate you from their company, and shall reproach you, and cast out your name as evil, for the Son of man's sake. Rejoice ye in that day, and leap for joy: for, behold, your reward is great in heaven: for in the like manner did their fathers unto the prophets. *(Luke 6:22–23)*

Leader: O God of Joy, in whom our eternal delight is well founded, grant us peace of mind as we walk this labyrinth. Help us to feel your presence and know your joy. Focus our minds and our spirits that we are filled with your presence and love.

THE LABYRINTH

The people now begin the labyrinth in whatever way is most practical for the space. When each person has completed the journey, they should stand or be seated in silent prayer until all are finished. The labyrinth courses may be followed in silence or in repeating the word "Joy" or phrase "Give us your joy" while walking. It is entirely appropriate, if desired, to play "Jesu, Joy of Man's Desire" while individuals journey the labyrinth.

Advent 3: Labyrinth Liturgy of Joy

OPTIONAL COMMUNION

Here may be added a celebration of the Holy Eucharist or Special Prayers.

THE PROCESSION INTO THE WORLD

Leader: O God of Joy, who told us that there is exceeding joy in the presence of the angels of God over one sinner that repenteth. Fill us with the joy of this Advent season. Prepare our hearts as a cradle for you, our King and Lord. Remind us that it is not through the material that we are filled, but by every word from you.

People: Jesus said "I say unto you, that likewise joy shall be in heaven over one sinner that repenteth, more than over ninety and nine just persons, which need no repentance" *(Luke 15:7)*. Help us to be filled with joy and repentance such that we come to share with all the saints and angels in your heavenly kingdom. *Amen.*

Leader: Verily, verily, I say unto you, That ye shall weep and lament, but the world shall rejoice: and ye shall be sorrowful, but your sorrow shall be turned into joy. *(John 16:20)*
Now the God of hope fill you with all joy and peace in believing, that ye may abound in hope, through the power of the Holy Ghost *(Romans 15:13)*. Look forward to Christ's birth. Remember that you were born for a purpose of loving and serving God. Share that love with all the world. *Amen.*

Leader: Go in peace and joy to love and serve the source of all our joy.
People: Thanks be to God.

Advent 4:
Labyrinth Liturgy of Love

If desired and possible in the space, the colors violet or royal blue are preferred for decorations, banners, ribbons, etc.

THE OPENING

The congregation gathers by the labyrinth and stands or sits in prayer and quiet contemplation.

Leader: Greater love has no one than this: to lay down one's life for one's friends. *(John 15:13)*

If feasible, the leader lights the candles of an Advent wreath at the entrance to the labyrinth.

Leader: One of the teachers of the law came and heard them debating. Noticing that Jesus had given them a good answer, he asked him, "Of all the commandments, which is the most important?" "The most important one," answered Jesus, "is this: 'Hear, O Israel: The Lord our God, the Lord is one. Love the Lord your God with all your heart and with all your soul and with all your mind and with all your strength.' The second is this: 'Love your neighbor as yourself.' There is no commandment greater than these."

Advent 4: Labyrinth Liturgy of Love

"Well said, teacher," the man replied. "You are right in saying that God is one and there is no other but him. To love him with all your heart, with all your understanding and with all your strength, and to love your neighbor as yourself is more important than all burnt offerings and sacrifices."

When Jesus saw that he had answered wisely, he said to him, "You are not far from the kingdom of God." And from then on no one dared ask him any more questions. (*Mark 12: 28–34*)

Together all say or sing responsively Psalm 139:

Leader:	O Lord, you have searched me and known me. You know when I sit down and when I rise up;
People:	you discern my thoughts from far away.
Leader:	You search out my path and my lying down
People:	and are acquainted with all my ways.
Leader:	Even before a word is on my tongue,
People:	O Lord, you know it completely.
Leader:	You hem me in, behind and before,
People:	and lay your hand upon me.
Leader:	Such knowledge is too wonderful for me;
People:	it is so high that I cannot attain it.
Leader:	Where can I go from your spirit?
People:	Or where can I flee from your presence?
Leader:	If I ascend to heaven, you are there;
People:	if I make my bed in Sheol, you are there.
Leader:	If I take the wings of the morning
People:	and settle at the farthest limits of the sea,

Advent

Leader:	even there your hand shall lead me,
People:	and your right hand shall hold me fast.
Leader:	If I say, "Surely the darkness shall cover me,
People:	and night wraps itself around me,"
Leader:	even the darkness is not dark to you;
People:	the night is as bright as the day, for darkness is as light to you.
Leader:	For it was you who formed my inward parts;
People:	you knit me together in my mother's womb.
Leader:	I praise you, for I am fearfully and wonderfully made.
People:	Wonderful are your works; that I know very well.
Leader:	My frame was not hidden from you, when I was being made in secret,
People:	intricately woven in the depths of the earth.
Leader:	Your eyes beheld my unformed substance. In your book were written
People:	all the days that were formed for me, when none of them as yet existed.
Leader:	How weighty to me are your thoughts, O God!
People:	How vast is the sum of them!
Leader:	I try to count them—they are more than the sand;
People:	I come to the end—I am still with you.
Leader:	O that you would kill the wicked, O God,
People:	and that the bloodthirsty would depart from me—
Leader:	those who speak of you maliciously
People:	and lift themselves up against you for evil!

Advent 4: Labyrinth Liturgy of Love

Leader: Do I not hate those who hate you, O Lord?
People: And do I not loathe those who rise up against you?

Leader: I hate them with perfect hatred;
People: I count them my enemies.

Leader: Search me, O God, and know my heart;
People: test me and know my thoughts

Leader: See if there is any wicked way in me,
People: and lead me in the way everlasting.

Leader The Lord be with you.
People And also with you.
Leader: Let us pray.

Together: Our Father, who art in heaven,
    hallowed be thy Name,
    thy kingdom come,
    thy will be done,
        on earth as it is in heaven.
Give us this day our daily bread.
And forgive us our trespasses,
    as we forgive those who trespass against us.
And lead us not into temptation,
    but deliver us from evil.
For thine is the kingdom, and the power, and the glory,
    for ever and ever. Amen.

Leader: O Lord, show your mercy upon us;
People: And grant us your salvation.

Leader: Guide our steps, O Lord, help us to come to that Holy Hill of your presence within our hearts. Let each course remove us from the pain and suffering that keeps us from fulfilling you commandment to love one another

Advent

as you love us. Help us to love one another as we learn to love you.

THE LABYRINTH

The people now begin the labyrinth in whatever way is most practical for the space. When each person has completed the journey, they should stand or be seated in silent prayer until all are finished. The labyrinth courses may be followed in silence or in repeating the word "Love" or phrase "Give us your love" while walking. Others should consider singing a hymn, such as "What Wondrous Love Is This, O My Soul."

OPTIONAL COMMUNION

Here may be added a celebration of the Holy Eucharist or the leader may read the following from Psalm 18:1–3:

> I will love thee, O Lord, my strength. The Lord *is* my rock, and my fortress, and my deliverer; my God, my strength, in whom I will trust; my buckler, and the horn of my salvation, *and* my high tower. I will call upon the Lord, *who is worthy* to be praised: so shall I be saved from mine enemies.

THE PROCESSION INTO THE WORLD

Leader: Enfold us in the wings of your love, O God. Help our feet and our hearts to lead us to you. Strengthen our love for one another so that we can love our enemies as much as our friends, knowing all to be your children and made in your image. Encourage us to see the miracle of the nativity and the boundless love for us

Advent 4: Labyrinth Liturgy of Love

that Jesus' birth represents. Help us to bring that love to all, ever in your Holy Name we pray. *Amen.*

Leader: Go in peace, hope, and joy to love and serve the incarnation of Love.
People: Thanks be to God.

Christmas Eve Labyrinth Liturgy

If desired and possible in the space, the colors white or gold are preferred for decorations, banners, ribbons, etc.

THE OPENING

The congregation gathers by the labyrinth and stands or sits in prayer and quiet contemplation. If candles are desired in the evening, they should be lit from the Advent Candles.

Leader: For God so loved the world that he gave his one and only Son, that whoever believes in him shall not perish but have eternal life. For God did not send his Son into the world to condemn the world, but to save the world through him. *(John 3:16–17)*

Dearly beloved, our time of waiting for God incarnate is nearly over. The advent anticipation like a breath about to be exhaled. Come to our own Bethlehem and be fed spiritually.

Reader: A reading from the First Chapter of the Gospel according to Luke, verses 26–38:
In the sixth month the angel Gabriel was sent by God to a town in Galilee called Nazareth, to a virgin

engaged to a man whose name was Joseph, of the house of David. The virgin's name was Mary. And he came to her and said, "Greetings, favored one! The Lord is with you." But she was much perplexed by his words and pondered what sort of greeting this might be. The angel said to her, "Do not be afraid, Mary, for you have found favor with God. And now, you will conceive in your womb and bear a son, and you will name him Jesus. He will be great, and will be called the Son of the Most High, and the Lord God will give to him the throne of his ancestor David. He will reign over the house of Jacob forever, and of his kingdom there will be no end." Mary said to the angel, "How can this be, since I am a virgin?" The angel said to her, "The Holy Spirit will come upon you, and the power of the Most High will overshadow you; therefore the child to be born will be holy; he will be called Son of God. And now, your relative Elizabeth in her old age has also conceived a son; and this is the sixth month for her who was said to be barren. For nothing will be impossible with God." Then Mary said, "Here am I, the servant of the Lord; let it be with me according to your word." Then the angel departed from her.
Here ends the reading.

Leader: Light of the World, be with us.
People: Light of the World, be with us.

If the service is in the evening, or inside a darkened space, candles may be given to each participant, lit from a common candle.

THE LABYRINTH

The people now begin the labyrinth in whatever way is most practical for the space, and holding their candles if provided. As the first

Advent

person begins the labyrinth, the leader begins reading Luke 1:39–46, 39–56

In those days Mary set out and went with haste to a Judean town in the hill country, where she entered the house of Zechariah and greeted Elizabeth. When Elizabeth heard Mary's greeting, the child leaped in her womb. And Elizabeth was filled with the Holy Spirit and exclaimed with a loud cry, "Blessed are you among women, and blessed is the fruit of your womb. And why has this happened to me, that the mother of my Lord comes to me? For as soon as I heard the sound of your greeting, the child in my womb leaped for joy. And blessed is she who believed that there would be a fulfillment of what was spoken to her by the Lord."

And Mary said,

> My soul magnifies the Lord,
>   and my spirit rejoices in God my Savior,
> for he has looked with favor on the lowliness of
>   his servant.
> Surely, from now on all generations will call me
>   blessed;
> for the Mighty One has done great things for me,
>   and holy is his name.
> His mercy is for those who fear him
>   from generation to generation.
> He has shown strength with his arm;
>   he has scattered the proud in the thoughts of
>   their hearts.
> He has brought down the powerful from their
>   thrones,
>   and lifted up the lowly;
> he has filled the hungry with good things,
>   and sent the rich away empty.
> He has helped his servant Israel,

>   in remembrance of his mercy,
>   according to the promise he made to our ancestors,
>   to Abraham and to his descendants forever."

> And Mary remained with her about three months and then returned to her home

OPTIONAL COMMUNION

Here may be added a celebration of the Holy Eucharist or the leader continues:

Leader	The Lord be with you.
People	And also with you.
Leader:	Let us pray.

Together: Our Father, who art in heaven,
> hallowed be thy Name,
> thy kingdom come,
> thy will be done,
>> on earth as it is in heaven.
>
> Give us this day our daily bread.
> And forgive us our trespasses,
>> as we forgive those who trespass against us.
>
> And lead us not into temptation,
>> but deliver us from evil.
>
> For thine is the kingdom, and the power, and the glory,
>> for ever and ever. Amen.

THE PROCESSION INTO THE WORLD

Leader: As Mary bore Jesus out of her faith and love of you, O God, our creator and perfect parent, strengthen us to bear your will and build your kingdom. Help our feet and our hearts to lead us to you. Strengthen our

Advent

love for one another so that we can love our enemies as much as our friends, knowing all to be your children and made in your image. Encourage us to see the miracle of the nativity and the boundless love for us that Jesus' birth represents. Help us to bring that love to all, ever in your Holy Name we pray. *Amen.*

Leader: Go in peace, hope, and joy to love and serve the incarnate Word.
People: Thanks be to God.

Christmastide

Christmas Labyrinth Liturgy

If desired and possible in the space, the colors white or gold are preferred for decorations, banners, ribbons, etc.

THE OPENING

The congregation gathers by the labyrinth and stands or sits in prayer and quiet contemplation. If candles are desired in the evening, they should be lit from the Advent Candles. The leader begins with this reading:

Leader: A reading from Luke 2:8–14
And in the same region there were shepherds out in the field, keeping watch over their flock by night. And an angel of the Lord appeared to them, and the glory of the Lord shone around them, and they were filled with great fear. And the angel said to them, "Fear not, for behold, I bring you good news of great joy that will be for all the people. For unto you is born this day in the city of David a Savior, who is Christ the Lord. And this will be a sign for you: you will find a baby wrapped in swaddling cloths and lying in a manger." And suddenly there was with the angel a multitude of the heavenly host praising God and saying,

Christmastide

"Glory to God in the highest, and on earth peace among those with whom He is pleased!"

Reader: When they saw the star, they rejoiced exceedingly with great joy. And going into the house, they saw the child with Mary his mother, and they fell down and worshiped him. Then, opening their treasures, they offered him gifts, gold and frankincense and myrrh. And being warned in a dream not to return to Herod, they departed to their own country by another way. *(Matthew 2:10–12)*

Leader: Worship the Lord, God with us! He has been born for our salvation.

THE LABYRINTH

The people now begin the labyrinth in whatever way is most practical for the space. If needed, a suggested prompt for prayer would be: "God is with us" or "Salvation has come." Christmas hymns may be sung as appropriate, but quietly.

OPTIONAL COMMUNION

Here may be added a celebration of the Holy Eucharist or the leader continues:

Leader The Lord be with you.
People And also with you.
Leader: Let us pray.

Together: Our Father, who art in heaven,
    hallowed be thy Name,
    thy kingdom come,
    thy will be done,

Christmas Labyrinth Liturgy

>on earth as it is in heaven.
Give us this day our daily bread.
And forgive us our trespasses,
>as we forgive those who trespass against us.
And lead us not into temptation,
>but deliver us from evil.
For thine is the kingdom, and the power, and the glory,
>for ever and ever. Amen.

THE PROCESSION INTO THE WORLD

Leader : You made yourself human to be with us and love us, O God. You came to live and die so that we might have eternal life. Bless all of us here present to serve you, that we might share your overwhelming love with all people in all places. The blessings of the incarnate God, our Mediator and Advocate, be with us all forevermore. *Amen.*

Leader: Go in peace, hope, and joy to love and serve our loving incarnate Lord.
People: Thanks be to God.

An Epiphany Liturgy of the Labyrinth

If desired and possible in the space, the color white is preferred for decorations, banners, ribbons, etc.

THE OPENING

The congregation gathers by the labyrinth and stands or sits in prayer and quiet contemplation.

Leader The Lord be with you.
People And also with you.

Leader: A reading from Matthew 2:1–12:
In the time of King Herod, after Jesus was born in Bethlehem of Judea, wise men from the East came to Jerusalem, asking, "Where is the child who has been born king of the Jews? For we observed his star at its rising, and have come to pay him homage." When King Herod heard this, he was frightened, and all Jerusalem with him; and calling together all the chief priests and scribes of the people, he inquired of them where the Messiah was to be born. They told him, "In Bethlehem of Judea; for so it has been written by the prophet:

'And you, Bethlehem, in the land of Judah,
are by no means least among the rulers of Judah;

An Epiphany Liturgy of the Labyrinth

for from you shall come a ruler
who is to shepherd my people Israel.'"
Then Herod secretly called for the wise men and learned from them the exact time when the star had appeared. Then he sent them to Bethlehem, saying, "Go and search diligently for the child; and when you have found him, bring me word so that I may also go and pay him homage." When they had heard the king, they set out; and there, ahead of them, went the star that they had seen at its rising, until it stopped over the place where the child was. When they saw that the star had stopped, they were overwhelmed with joy. On entering the house, they saw the child with Mary his mother; and they knelt down and paid him homage. Then, opening their treasure chests, they offered him gifts of gold, frankincense, and myrrh. And having been warned in a dream not to return to Herod, they left for their own country by another road.

Or this from the John 2:1-11.

And the third day there was a marriage in Cana of Galilee; and the mother of Jesus was there: And both Jesus was called, and his disciples, to the marriage. And when they wanted wine, the mother of Jesus saith unto him, They have no wine. Jesus saith unto her, Woman, what have I to do with thee? mine hour is not yet come. His mother saith unto the servants, Whatsoever he saith unto you, do it. And there were set there six waterpots of stone, after the manner of the purifying of the Jews, containing two or three firkins apiece. Jesus saith unto them, Fill the waterpots with water. And they filled them up to the brim. And he saith unto them, Draw out now, and bear unto the governor of the feast. And they bare it. When the ruler of the feast had tasted the water that was made wine, and knew not whence it was: (but the servants which

Christmastide

drew the water knew;) the governor of the feast called the bridegroom, And saith unto him, Every man at the beginning doth set forth good wine; and when men have well drunk, then that which is worse: but thou hast kept the good wine until now. This beginning of miracles did Jesus in Cana of Galilee, and manifested forth his glory; and his disciples believed on him.

Leader   The Word of the Lord.
People   Thanks be to God.

Leader   Seek ye first the kingdom of God, and his righteousness; and all these things shall be added unto you. (*Matthew 6:33*)
People   The LORD makes firm the steps of the one who delights in him. (*Psalm 37:23*)
Leader   He guides the humble in what is right and teaches them his way. (*Psalm 25:9*)
People   Since you are my rock and my fortress, for the sake of your name lead and guide me. (*Psalm 31:3*)

Leader   God has prepared a place to walk along his holy way. Let us praise God and seek the purity of heart to listen and follow.

THE LABYRINTH

The people now begin the labyrinth in whatever way is most practical for the space, and holding their candles if provided. An appropriate hymn or anthem may quietly be sung if desired. If desired, a phrase like the following may be repeated:

> Light of the world, reveal yourself in my life and let me truly see you.

An Epiphany Liturgy of the Labyrinth

OPTIONAL COMMUNION

Here may be added a celebration of the Holy Eucharist or the leader continues:

Leader   The Lord be with you.
People   And also with you.
Leader: Let us pray.

Together: Our Father, who art in heaven,
        hallowed be thy Name,
        thy kingdom come,
        thy will be done,
            on earth as it is in heaven.
    Give us this day our daily bread.
    And forgive us our trespasses,
        as we forgive those who trespass against us.
    And lead us not into temptation,
        but deliver us from evil.
    For thine is the kingdom, and the power, and the glory,
        for ever and ever. Amen.

THE PROCESSION INTO THE WORLD

Leader   As God appeared before Moses at the burning bush, and Christ was revealed to the world by Magi, at Cana, and at his baptism, let us remember that God is with us always. His Holy Spirit is present and enfolds us in love and peace. Share that love, peace, and presence with the world, now and always.

Leader: Go in peace, hope, and joy to love and serve the Source of all wisdom, who appears to us in times of need.
People: Thanks be to God.

Between Christmastide
and Holy Week

Figure 4. Baptism at Chartres, inspired by da Vinci. © Rob Elsner

A Liturgy for the Baptism of the Lord

If desired and possible in the space, the color white is preferred for decorations, banners, ribbons, etc.

THE OPENING

The congregation gathers by the labyrinth and stands or sits in prayer and quiet contemplation. The leader or a member of the congregation begins with this reading from

Leader: The Lord be with you.
People: And also with you.

Leader: A reading from Matthew 3:13–17 (NRSV)
Then Jesus came from Galilee to John at the Jordan, to be baptized by him. John would have prevented him, saying, "I need to be baptized by you, and do you come to me?" But Jesus answered him, "Let it be so now; for it is proper for us in this way to fulfill all righteousness." Then he consented. And when Jesus had been baptized, just as he came up from the water, suddenly the heavens were opened to him and he saw the Spirit of God descending like a dove and alighting on him. And a voice from heaven said, "This is my Son, the Beloved, with whom I am well pleased."

Between Christmastide and Holy Week

THE RENEWAL OF BAPTISMAL VOWS

Leader: As Jesus arose from the water he was anointed by the Spirit of God and proclaimed as God's Son. We too are anointed by that same Spirit; reborn and adopted as sons and daughters with whom God is well pleased. As we celebrate the feast of our Lord's Baptism, let us renew our own baptismal covenant.

Leader: Do you reaffirm your renunciation of evil and renew your commitment to Jesus Christ?

People: I do.

Leader: Do you believe in God the Father?

People: I believe in God, the Father almighty, creator of heaven and earth.

Leader: Do you believe in Jesus Christ, the Son of God?

People: I believe in Jesus Christ, his only Son, our Lord. He was conceived by the power of the Holy Spirit and born of the Virgin Mary. He suffered under Pontius Pilate, was crucified, died, and was buried. He descended to the dead. On the third day he rose again. He ascended into heaven, and is seated at the right hand of the Father. He will come again to judge the living and the dead.

Leader: Do you believe in God the Holy Spirit?

People: I believe in the Holy Spirit, the holy catholic church, the communion of saints, the forgiveness of sins, the resurrection of the body, and the life everlasting.

Leader: Will you continue in the apostles' teaching and fellowship, in the breaking of bread, and in the prayers?

People: I will, with God's help.

Leader: Will you persevere in resisting evil, and, whenever you fall into sin, repent and return to the Lord?

People: I will, with God's help.

Leader: Will you proclaim by word and example the good news of God in Christ?

People: I will, with God's help.

A Liturgy for the Baptism of the Lord

Leader: Will you seek and serve Christ in all persons, loving your neighbor as yourself?
People: I will, with God's help.
Leader: Will you strive for justice and peace among all people, and respect the dignity of every human being?
People: I will, with God's help.
Leader: May Almighty God, the Father of our Lord Jesus Christ, who has given us a new birth by water and the Holy Spirit, and bestowed upon us the forgiveness of sins, keep us in eternal life by his grace, in Christ Jesus our Lord. As we walk the labyrinth, let us focus our minds and hearts upon him and the example he set for us. *Amen.*

THE LABYRINTH

The people now begin the labyrinth in whatever way is most practical for the space. An appropriate hymn or anthem may quietly be sung if desired. If in need of a repeating prayer, please consider this:

> Wash my heart of all sin and doubt, O Lord, and let me fully serve you.

OPTIONAL COMMUNION

Here may be added a celebration of the Holy Eucharist or the leader continues:

Leader: The Lord be with you.
People: And also with you.
Leader: Let us pray.

Together: Our Father, who art in heaven,
hallowed be thy Name,
thy kingdom come,

Between Christmastide and Holy Week

> thy will be done,
> on earth as it is in heaven.
> Give us this day our daily bread.
> And forgive us our trespasses,
> as we forgive those who trespass against us.
> And lead us not into temptation,
> but deliver us from evil.
> For thine is the kingdom, and the power, and the glory,
> for ever and ever. Amen.

THE PROCESSION INTO THE WORLD

Leader: As God revealed Jesus to the world as the Divine Son, let us humbly thank God for the blessing of forgiveness and love. Remember that you are God's beloved children. Love one another and share the joy of God's love with all. And the blessings of Father, Son, and Holy Spirit be with us all evermore. *Amen.*

Leader: Go in peace, hope, and joy to love and serve the Lord, the Living Water.
People: Thanks be to God.

A Liturgy for the Transfiguration

If desired and possible in the space, the color white is preferred for decorations, banners, ribbons, etc.

THE OPENING

The congregation gathers by the labyrinth and stands or sits in prayer and quiet contemplation. The leader or a member of the congregation begins with this:

Reader: A reading from Matthew 17:1–13
    Six days later, Jesus took with him Peter and James and his brother John and led them up a high mountain, by themselves. And he was transfigured before them, and his face shone like the sun, and his clothes became dazzling white. Suddenly there appeared to them Moses and Elijah, talking with him. Then Peter said to Jesus, "Lord, it is good for us to be here; if you wish, I will make three dwellings here, one for you, one for Moses, and one for Elijah." While he was still speaking, suddenly a bright cloud overshadowed them, and from the cloud a voice said, "This is my Son, the Beloved; with him I am well pleased; listen to him!" When the disciples heard this, they fell to the ground and were overcome by fear. But Jesus came and

touched them, saying, "Get up and do not be afraid." And when they looked up, they saw no one except Jesus himself alone. As they were coming down the mountain, Jesus ordered them, "Tell no one about the vision until after the Son of Man has been raised from the dead." And the disciples asked him, "Why, then, do the scribes say that Elijah must come first?" He replied, "Elijah is indeed coming and will restore all things; but I tell you that Elijah has already come, and they did not recognize him, but they did to him whatever they pleased. So also the Son of Man is about to suffer at their hands." Then the disciples understood that he was speaking to them about John the Baptist.

The word of the Lord

People   Thanks be to God.

Leader: Let us pray. O Lord, bless us your people so that we may see you in our lives.
People   Lord, transform our hearts and minds.
Leader   Bless all the countries of the earth, and let peace prevail among all people.
People   Lord, transform our hearts and minds.
Leader   Strengthen us to withstand doubt and fear and walk in your ways.
People   Lord, transform our hearts and minds.
Leader   Help us to understand you, O God, and write your laws in our hearts.
People   Lord, transform our hearts and minds.

THE LABYRINTH

The people now begin the labyrinth in whatever way is most practical for the space. An appropriate hymn or anthem may quietly be

A Liturgy for the Transfiguration

sung if desired. Focus on the humanity and divinity of Jesus should be emphasized. If needed, consider repeating this prayer:

> Help me to know and understand you, my Lord and my God.

OPTIONAL COMMUNION

Here may be added a celebration of the Holy Eucharist or the leader continues:

Leader: The Lord be with you.
People: And also with you.
Leader: Let us pray.

Together: Our Father, who art in heaven,
hallowed be thy Name,
thy kingdom come,
thy will be done,
on earth as it is in heaven.
Give us this day our daily bread.
And forgive us our trespasses,
as we forgive those who trespass against us.
And lead us not into temptation,
but deliver us from evil.
For thine is the kingdom, and the power, and the glory,
for ever and ever. Amen.

THE PROCESSION INTO THE WORLD

Leader: O Christ, you showed yourself with Moses and Elijah to Peter, James, and John, let us know you and see you in our lives. Help us to ever remember that you were fully human, yet also fully divine. Overwhelm us with your radiant love and transfigure our hearts and minds

Between Christmastide and Holy Week

to love and serve you and be kinder to one another. In your Holy Name we pray. *Amen.*

Leader: Go in peace, hope, and joy to love and serve the Lord.
People: Thanks be to God.

A Lenten Liturgy of the Labyrinth

The term Lent comes from an old word meaning a lengthening of days. Lent is a season of preparation and humility. It is a time where we repent of our sins and seek ways to avoiding sins in the future.

If desired and possible in the space, the color violet (or unbleached linen) is preferred for decorations, banners, ribbons, etc. On the fourth or middle Sunday, also called Laetare[1] Sunday, pink may be used.

THE OPENING

The congregation gathers by the labyrinth and stands or sits in prayer and quiet contemplation. The leader begins with this reading.

Leader: There Elijah entered a cave and spent the night. And the word of the LORD came to him, saying, "What are you doing here, Elijah?"
"I have been very zealous for the LORD, the God of Hosts," he replied, "but the Israelites have forsaken Your covenant, torn down Your altars, and killed Your prophets with the sword. I am the only one left, and they are seeking my life as well."

---

1. *Laetare* is another Latin word for "Rejoice," and is the word that started the Mass in the Roman Church.

Then the Lord said, "Go out and stand on the mountain before the Lord. Behold, the Lord is about to pass by."

And a great and mighty wind tore into the mountains and shattered the rocks before the Lord, but the Lord was not in the wind.

After the wind there was an earthquake, but the Lord was not in the earthquake.

After the earthquake there was a fire, but the Lord was not in the fire.

And after the fire came a still, small voice. When Elijah heard it, he wrapped his face in his cloak and went out and stood at the mouth of the cave. Suddenly a voice came to him and said, "What are you doing here, Elijah?" *(1 Kings 19:9–13)*

THE LABYRINTH

The people now begin the labyrinth in whatever way is most practical for the space. As the first person begins the labyrinth, the leader may read Psalm 51:

> Have mercy on me, O God,
>   according to your steadfast love;
> according to your abundant mercy,
>   blot out my transgressions.
> Wash me thoroughly from my iniquity,
>   and cleanse me from my sin.
> For I know my transgressions,
>   and my sin is ever before me.
> Against you, you alone, have I sinned
>   and done what is evil in your sight,
> so that you are justified in your sentence
>   and blameless when you pass judgment.
> Indeed, I was born guilty,
>   a sinner when my mother conceived me.

A Lenten Liturgy of the Labyrinth

You desire truth in the inward being;
    therefore teach me wisdom in my secret heart.
Purge me with hyssop, and I shall be clean;
    wash me, and I shall be whiter than snow.
Let me hear joy and gladness;
    let the bones that you have crushed rejoice.
Hide your face from my sins,
    and blot out all my iniquities.
Create in me a clean heart, O God,
    and put a new and right spirit within me.
Do not cast me away from your presence,
    and do not take your holy spirit from me.
Restore to me the joy of your salvation,
    and sustain in me a willing spirit.
Then I will teach transgressors your ways,
    and sinners will return to you.
Deliver me from bloodshed, O God,
    O God of my salvation,
    and my tongue will sing aloud of your deliverance.
O Lord, open my lips,
    and my mouth will declare your praise.
For you have no delight in sacrifice;
    if I were to give a burnt offering, you would not be pleased.
The sacrifice acceptable to God is a broken spirit;
    a broken and contrite heart, O God, you will not despise.
Do good to Zion in your good pleasure;
    rebuild the walls of Jerusalem;
then you will delight in right sacrifices,
    in burnt offerings and whole burnt offerings;
then bulls will be offered on your altar.

Between Christmastide and Holy Week

OPTIONAL COMMUNION

Here may be added a celebration of the Holy Eucharist or the leader continues:

Leader: The Lord be with you.
People: And also with you.
Leader: Let us pray.

Together: Our Father, who art in heaven,
hallowed be thy Name,
thy kingdom come,
thy will be done,
on earth as it is in heaven.
Give us this day our daily bread.
And forgive us our trespasses,
as we forgive those who trespass against us.
And lead us not into temptation,
but deliver us from evil.
For thine is the kingdom, and the power, and the glory,
for ever and ever. Amen.

THE PROCESSION INTO THE WORLD

Leader: If we say that we have no sin, we deceive ourselves, and the truth is not in us. If we confess our sins, he who is faithful and just will forgive us our sins and cleanse us from all unrighteousness. If we say that we have not sinned, we make him a liar, and his word is not in us. (1 John 1:8–10)

Be blessed by the one who made you and loves you as you are. Repent and forgive others. And the blessings of Father, Son, and Holy Spirit be on us all, now and always. Amen.

A Lenten Liturgy of the Labyrinth

Leader: Go in peace and prayer to love and serve the Lord.
People: Thanks be to God.

Holy Week and Easter

Figure 5. Jesus' entrance to Jerusalem at Canterbury,
inspired by van Dyck. © Rob Elsner

A Palm Sunday Liturgy of the Labyrinth

If desired and possible in the space, the color red is preferred for decorations, banners, ribbons, etc.

THE OPENING

The congregation gathers by the labyrinth and stands or sits in prayer and quiet contemplation. The leader begins with this reading:

Leader: The great crowd that had come to the festival heard that Jesus was coming to Jerusalem. So they took branches of palm trees and went out to meet him, shouting, "Hosanna! Blessed is the one who comes in the name of the Lord—the King of Israel!" Jesus found a young donkey and sat on it; as it is written: "Do not be afraid, daughter of Zion. Look, your king is coming, sitting on a donkey's colt!" His disciples did not understand these things at first; but when Jesus was glorified, then they remembered that these things had been written of him and had been done to him. (*John 12:12–16*)

Leader: The Gospel of the Lord. Hosanna!
People: Praise to you, Lord Christ. Hosanna in the highest!

Holy Week and Easter

Leader: The Lord be with you.
People And also with you.
Leader: Let us give thanks to the Lord our God.
People: It is right to give God thanks and praise.
Leader: We thank you and praise you, Almighty God, for the overwhelming love you give us and by which you redeemed us through your Son. On this day Jesus entered the holy city of Jerusalem in triumph, and was proclaimed as King of kings by those who spread their garments and branches of palm along his way. Let the branches we carry through this labyrinth be for us signs of his victory and reminders of his carrying the cross for our salvation. Grant that we who bear them in his name may ever hail him as our King, and follow him in the way that leads to eternal life; who lives and reigns in glory with you and the Holy Spirit, now and for ever. Amen.
Leader: Blessed is he who comes in the name of the Lord.
People: Hosanna in the highest!

THE LABYRINTH

A foot washing is appropriate, possibly using the suggested form on pp. 132–34. The people now begin the labyrinth in whatever way is most practical for the space, carrying palms if at all possible. Songs of praise and hosannas may be sung.

OPTIONAL COMMUNION

Here may be added a celebration of the Holy Eucharist or the following:

Leader: Therefore God also highly exalted him and gave him the name that is above every name, so that at the name of Jesus every knee should bend, in heaven and on

A Palm Sunday Liturgy of the Labyrinth

earth and under the earth, and every tongue should confess that Jesus Christ is Lord, to the glory of God the Father. *(Philippians 2: 9–11)*

THE PROCESSION INTO THE WORLD

Leader: All hail our King, who comes in humility to save us from sin and death. Throw cloaks and palms on the road. Let us welcome him into our hearts and homes, now and always. *Amen.*

Leader: Go in peace, hope, and joy to love and serve the King of Creation, ruler of our hearts.

People: Thanks be to God.

An Ash Wednesday Liturgy of the Labyrinth

If desired and possible in the space, the color violet (or unbleached linen) is preferred for decorations, banners, ribbons, etc.

THE OPENING

The congregation gathers by the labyrinth and stands or sits in prayer and quiet contemplation.

Leader: Beware of practicing your piety before others in order to be seen by them; for then you have no reward from your Father in heaven. So whenever you give alms, do not sound a trumpet before you, as the hypocrites do in the synagogues and in the streets, so that they may be praised by others. Truly I tell you, they have received their reward. But when you give alms, do not let your left hand know what your right hand is doing, so that your alms may be done in secret; and your Father who sees in secret will reward you. And whenever you pray, do not be like the hypocrites; for they love to stand and pray in the synagogues and at the street corners, so that they may be seen by others. Truly I tell you, they have received their reward. But whenever you pray, go into your room and shut the door and pray to your Father who is in secret; and your Father who sees in secret will reward you. And whenever you fast, do not look dismal, like the hypocrites, for they disfigure their faces so as to show others that they are fasting. Truly I tell you, they have received their reward. But when you fast, put oil on your head and wash your face, so that your fasting may be seen not by others but by your Father who is in secret; and your Father who sees in secret will reward you. Do not store up for yourselves treasures on earth, where moth and rust consume and where thieves break in and steal; but store up for yourselves treasures in heaven, where neither moth nor rust consumes and where thieves do not break in and steal. For where your treasure is, there your heart will be also. *(Matthew 6:1–6, 16–21)*

Leader: O God, who sees into our secret heart, cleanse us from all sin, forgive us our weaknesses and failings when we do not follow you and your loving word.
People: Give us your mercy, Lord, for we have not kept all your commandments.
Leader: O Father, who holds us through tears and delights, enable us to see salvation.
People: Give us your mercy, Lord, for we have fallen short of your glory.
Leader: O Christ, who suffered for us and arose to give us faith and hope, give us ever more hope and a deeper faith.
People: Give us your mercy, Lord, for we need your love.
Leader: O Spirit, who travels with us every day of our life, empower us to live and walk in your ways.
People: Give us your mercy, Lord, for we have fallen short of your glory.

Holy Week and Easter

THE LABYRINTH

A foot washing is appropriate, possibly using the suggested form on pp. 132–34. The people now begin the labyrinth in whatever way is most practical for the space. As the first person begins the labyrinth, the leader begins reading Psalm 51, at least verses 1–17.

> Have mercy on me, O God, according to your steadfast love; according to your abundant mercy blot out my transgressions. Wash me thoroughly from my iniquity, and cleanse me from my sin. For I know my transgressions, and my sin is ever before me. Against you, you alone, have I sinned, and done what is evil in your sight, so that you are justified in your sentence and blameless when you pass judgment. Indeed, I was born guilty, a sinner when my mother conceived me. You desire truth in the inward being; therefore teach me wisdom in my secret heart. Purge me with hyssop, and I shall be clean; wash me, and I shall be whiter than snow. Let me hear joy and gladness; let the bones that you have crushed rejoice. Hide your face from my sins, and blot out all my iniquities. Create in me a clean heart, O God, and put a new and right spirit within me. Do not cast me away from your presence, and do not take your holy spirit from me. Restore to me the joy of your salvation, and sustain in me a willing spirit. Then I will teach transgressors your ways, and sinners will return to you. Deliver me from bloodshed, O God, O God of my salvation, and my tongue will sing aloud of your deliverance. O Lord, open my lips, and my mouth will declare your praise. For you have no delight in sacrifice; if I were to give a burnt offering, you would not be pleased. The sacrifice acceptable to God is a broken spirit; a broken and contrite heart, O God, you will not despise.

OPTIONAL COMMUNION AND IMPOSITION OF ASHES

Here may be added a celebration of the Holy Eucharist and imposition of ashes or the leader continues:

Leader: The Lord be with you.
People: And also with you.
Leader: Let us pray.

Leader: O Merciful God, who gave himself for us, be with us. Allow us to truly be humble before you and your people. Cleanse our hearts of all sin, and direct us in your ways that we may come to truly know you and love you even more than we love ourselves. *Amen.*

Together: Our Father, who art in heaven,
> hallowed be thy Name,
> thy kingdom come,
> thy will be done,
>> on earth as it is in heaven.
> Give us this day our daily bread.
> And forgive us our trespasses,
>> as we forgive those who trespass against us.
> And lead us not into temptation,
>> but deliver us from evil.
> For thine is the kingdom, and the power, and the glory,
>> for ever and ever. Amen.

THE PROCESSION INTO THE WORLD

Leader: May God bless us and keep us. May the Lord of love, peace, and mercy be with us. May all soiling of our spirits be cleansed, and humility and purity redefine our lives. And may the blessing of Father, Son, and Holy Spirit be with us all evermore. *Amen.*

Holy Week and Easter

Leader: Go in peace, hope, and joy to love and serve the Lord.
People: Thanks be to God.

A Maundy Thursday Liturgy of the Labyrinth

If desired and possible in the space, the color red is preferred for decorations, banners, ribbons, etc.

THE OPENING

The congregation gathers by the labyrinth and stands or sits in prayer and quiet contemplation. The leader begins with this reading from Psalm 116:1–2, 12–19

Leader: I love the Lord, because he has heard my voice and my supplications.

People: Because he inclined his ear to me, therefore I will call on him as long as I live.

Leader: What shall I return to the Lord for all his bounty to me?

People: I will lift up the cup of salvation and call on the name of the Lord,

Leader: I will pay my vows to the Lord in the presence of all his people.

People: Precious in the sight of the Lord is the death of his faithful ones.

Leader: O Lord, I am your servant; I am your servant, the child of your serving girl.

Holy Week and Easter

People: You have loosed my bonds.
Leader: I will offer to you a thanksgiving sacrifice and call on the name of the Lord.
People: I will pay my vows to the Lord in the presence of all his people,
Leader: in the courts of the house of the Lord, in your midst, O Jerusalem.
People: Praise the Lord!

Leader: The Gospel according to John from the 13th chapter, verses 1–17 and 31–35.
Now before the festival of the Passover, Jesus knew that his hour had come to depart from this world and go to the Father. Having loved his own who were in the world, he loved them to the end. The devil had already put it into the heart of Judas son of Simon Iscariot to betray him. And during supper Jesus, knowing that the Father had given all things into his hands, and that he had come from God and was going to God, got up from the table, took off his outer robe, and tied a towel around himself. Then he poured water into a basin and began to wash the disciples' feet and to wipe them with the towel that was tied around him. He came to Simon Peter, who said to him, "Lord, are you going to wash my feet?" Jesus answered, "You do not know now what I am doing, but later you will understand." Peter said to him, "You will never wash my feet." Jesus answered, "Unless I wash you, you have no share with me." Simon Peter said to him, "Lord, not my feet only but also my hands and my head!" Jesus said to him, "One who has bathed does not need to wash, except for the feet, but is entirely clean. And you are clean, though not all of you." For he knew who was to betray him; for this reason he said, "Not all of you are clean." After he had washed their feet, had put on his robe, and had returned to the table, he said to them, "Do you know

A Maundy Thursday Liturgy of the Labyrinth

what I have done to you? You call me Teacher and Lord—and you are right, for that is what I am. So if I, your Lord and Teacher, have washed your feet, you also ought to wash one another's feet. For I have set you an example, that you also should do as I have done to you. Very truly, I tell you, servants are not greater than their master, nor are messengers greater than the one who sent them. If you know these things, you are blessed if you do them." When he had gone out, Jesus said, "Now the Son of Man has been glorified, and God has been glorified in him. If God has been glorified in him, God will also glorify him in himself and will glorify him at once. Little children, I am with you only a little longer. You will look for me; and as I said to the Jews so now I say to you, 'Where I am going, you cannot come.' I give you a new commandment, that you love one another. Just as I have loved you, you also should love one another. By this everyone will know that you are my disciples, if you have love for one another."

Leader: The Gospel of the Lord
People: Praise to you, Lord Christ

THE LABYRINTH

A foot washing is appropriate, possibly using the suggested form on pp. 132–34. The people now begin the labyrinth in whatever way is most practical for the space. If possible, silence should be kept except the quite prayers of those present. A repeated prayer for this journey might be:

> Let me serve others with grace and humility, and accept them serving me the same way.

Holy Week and Easter

OPTIONAL COMMUNION

Here may be added a celebration of the Holy Eucharist or a reader may read the following from Exodus 12:1–4, (5–10), 11–14:

> The LORD said to Moses and Aaron in the land of Egypt: This month shall mark for you the beginning of months; it shall be the first month of the year for you. Tell the whole congregation of Israel that on the tenth of this month they are to take a lamb for each family, a lamb for each household. If a household is too small for a whole lamb, it shall join its closest neighbor in obtaining one; the lamb shall be divided in proportion to the number of people who eat of it. Your lamb shall be without blemish, a year-old male; you may take it from the sheep or from the goats. You shall keep it until the fourteenth day of this month; then the whole assembled congregation of Israel shall slaughter it at twilight. They shall take some of the blood and put it on the two doorposts and the lintel of the houses in which they eat it. They shall eat the lamb that same night; they shall eat it roasted over the fire with unleavened bread and bitter herbs. Do not eat any of it raw or boiled in water, but roasted over the fire, with its head, legs, and inner organs. You shall let none of it remain until the morning; anything that remains until the morning you shall burn. This is how you shall eat it: your loins girded, your sandals on your feet, and your staff in your hand; and you shall eat it hurriedly. It is the Passover of the LORD. For I will pass through the land of Egypt that night, and I will strike down every firstborn in the land of Egypt, both human beings and animals; on all the gods of Egypt I will execute judgments: I am the LORD. The blood shall be a sign for you on the houses where you live: when I see the blood, I will pass over you, and no plague shall destroy you when I strike the land of Egypt. This day shall be a

day of remembrance for you. You shall celebrate it as a festival to the LORD; throughout your generations you shall observe it as a perpetual ordinance.

THE PROCESSION INTO THE WORLD

Leader: Blessed are the feet of the messengers who bring us the gospel of peace. May the Spirit of Light and Life shine on your path. May the God of Love and Kindness who led Israel to the promised land guide you to peace. May the Son who washed feet as a servant rule over our hearts so that we may serve others. And the blessings of God, Father, Son, and Holy Spirit be with you now and always. *Amen.*

Leader: Go in peace, hope, and joy to love and serve the Lamb who lays down his life for us.
People: Thanks be to God.

Figure 6. Crucifixion at Saint Stephen's, Vestavia Hills, Alabama, inspired by Grunwald. © Rob Elsner

A Good Friday Liturgy of the Labyrinth

If desired and possible in the space, the colors black or red are preferred for decorations, banners, ribbons, etc.

THE OPENING

The congregation gathers by the labyrinth and stands or sits in prayer and quiet contemplation.

Leader: But this is the covenant that I will make with the house of Israel after those days, says the LORD: I will put my law within them, and I will write it on their hearts; and I will be their God, and they shall be my people. *(Jeremiah 31:33)*

Leader: God spoke these words, and said: I am the LORD thy God; Thou shalt have none other gods but me.

People: Lord, have mercy upon us, and incline our hearts to keep this law.

Leader: Thou shalt not make to thyself any graven image, nor the likeness of any thing that is in heaven above, or in the earth beneath, or in the water under the earth; thou shalt not bow down to them, nor worship them: for I the LORD thy God am a jealous God, and visit the

	sins of the fathers upon the children, unto the third and fourth generation of them that hate me; and show mercy unto thousands in them that love me and keep my commandments.
People:	Lord, have mercy upon us, and incline our hearts to keep this law.
Leader:	Thou shalt not take the Name of the Lord thy God in vain; for the Lord will not hold him guiltless, that taketh his Name in vain.
People:	Lord, have mercy upon us, and incline our hearts to keep this law.
Leader:	Remember that thou keep holy the Sabbath-day. Six days shalt thou labour, and do all that thou hast to do; but the seventh day is the Sabbath of the Lord thy God. In it thou shalt do no manner of work; thou, and thy son, and thy daughter, thy man-servant, and thy maid-servant, thy cattle, and the stranger that is within thy gates. For in six days the Lord made heaven and earth, the sea, and all that in them is, and rested the seventh day: wherefore the Lord blessed the seventh day, and hallowed it.
People:	Lord, have mercy upon us, and incline our hearts to keep this law.
Leader:	Honor thy father and thy mother; that thy days may be long in the land which the Lord thy God giveth thee.
People:	Lord, have mercy upon us, and incline our hearts to keep this law.
Leader:	Thou shalt do no murder.

A Good Friday Liturgy of the Labyrinth

People: Lord, have mercy upon us, and incline our hearts to keep this law.

Leader: Thou shalt not commit adultery.
People: Lord, have mercy upon us, and incline our hearts to keep this law.

Leader: Thou shalt not steal.
People: Lord, have mercy upon us, and incline our hearts to keep this law.

Leader: Thou shalt not bear false witness against thy neighbor.
People: Lord, have mercy upon us, and incline our hearts to keep this law.

Leader: Thou shalt not covet thy neighbor's house, thou shalt not covet thy neighbor's wife, nor his servant, nor his maid, nor his ox, nor his ass, nor any thing that is his.

People: Lord, have mercy upon us, and write all these thy laws in our hearts, we beseech thee.

Leader: Hear what our Lord Jesus Christ saith. Thou shalt love the Lord thy God with all thy heart, and with all thy soul, and with all thy mind. This is the first and great commandment. And the second is like unto it; Thou shalt love thy neighbor as thyself. On these two commandments hang all the Law and the Prophets.

THE LABYRINTH

A foot washing is appropriate, possibly using the suggested form on pp. 132–34. The people now begin the labyrinth in whatever way is most practical for the space. As the first person begins the labyrinth, the leader begins reading Psalm 22.

Holy Week and Easter

My God, my God, why have you forsaken me?
> Why are you so far from helping me, from the words of my groaning?

O my God, I cry by day, but you do not answer;
> and by night but find no rest.

Yet you are holy,
> enthroned on the praises of Israel.

In you our ancestors trusted;
> they trusted, and you delivered them.

To you they cried and were saved;
> in you they trusted and were not put to shame.

But I am a worm and not human,
> scorned by others and despised by the people.

All who see me mock me;
> they sneer at me; they shake their heads;

"Commit your cause to the LORD; let him deliver—
> let him rescue the one in whom he delights!"

Yet it was you who took me from the womb;
> you kept me safe on my mother's breast.

On you I was cast from my birth,
> and since my mother bore me you have been my God.

Do not be far from me,
> for trouble is near,
> and there is no one to help.

Many bulls encircle me;
> strong bulls of Bashan surround me;

they open wide their mouths at me,
> like a ravening and roaring lion.

I am poured out like water,
> and all my bones are out of joint;

my heart is like wax;
> it is melted within my breast;

my mouth is dried up like a potsherd,
> and my tongue sticks to my jaws;
> you lay me in the dust of death.

A Good Friday Liturgy of the Labyrinth

For dogs are all around me;
    a company of evildoers encircles me;
they bound my hands and feet.
    I can count all my bones.
They stare and gloat over me;
    they divide my clothes among themselves,
    and for my clothing they cast lots.
But you, O Lord, do not be far away!
    O my help, come quickly to my aid!
Deliver my soul from the sword,
    my life from the power of the dog!
Save me from the mouth of the lion!
    From the horns of the wild oxen you have
    rescued me.
I will tell of your name to my brothers and sisters,
    in the midst of the congregation I will praise you:
You who fear the Lord, praise him!
    All you offspring of Jacob, glorify him;
    stand in awe of him, all you offspring of Israel!
For he did not despise or abhor
    the affliction of the afflicted;
he did not hide his face from me
    but heard when I cried to him.
From you comes my praise in the great congregation;
    my vows I will pay before those who fear him.
The poor shall eat and be satisfied;
    those who seek him shall praise the Lord.
    May your hearts live forever!
All the ends of the earth shall remember
    and turn to the Lord,
and all the families of the nations
    shall worship before him.
For dominion belongs to the Lord,
    and he rules over the nations.
To him, indeed, shall all who sleep in the earth bow down;

Holy Week and Easter

> before him shall bow all who go down to the dust,
> and I shall live for him.
> Posterity will serve him;
> future generations will be told about the LORD
> and proclaim his deliverance to a people yet unborn,
> saying that he has done it.

OPTIONAL COMMUNION

Here may be added a celebration of the Holy Eucharist or the leader continues:

Leader: The Lord be with you.
People: And with thy spirit.
Leader: Let us pray.

Together: I believe in one God the Father Almighty, Maker of heaven and earth, and of all things visible and invisible:
And in one Lord Jesus Christ, the only-begotten Son of God; begotten of his Father before all worlds, God of God, Light of Light, very God of very God; begotten, not made; being of one substance with the Father; by whom all things were made: who for us and for our salvation came down from heaven, and was incarnate by the Holy Ghost of the Virgin Mary, and was made man: and was crucified also for us under Pontius Pilate; he suffered and was buried: and the third day he rose again according to the Scriptures: and ascended into heaven, and sitteth on the right hand of the Father: and he shall come again, with glory, to judge both the quick and the dead; whose kingdom shall have no end.
And I believe in the Holy Ghost, the Lord, and Giver of Life, who proceedeth from the Father and the Son; who with the Father and the Son together is worshipped and glorified; who spake by the prophets:

and I believe one catholic and apostolic church: I acknowledge one baptism for the remission of sins: and I look for the resurrection of the dead: And the life of the world to come. Amen.

THE PROCESSION INTO THE WORLD

Leader: Love does no wrong to a neighbor; therefore, love is the fulfilling of the law. (*Romans 13:10*)

Together: O, Almighty Lord, and everlasting God, vouchsafe, we beseech thee, to direct, sanctify, and govern, both our hearts and bodies, in the ways of thy laws, and in the works of thy commandments; that, through thy most mighty protection, both here and ever, we may be preserved in body and soul; through our Lord and Savior Jesus Christ. Amen.

Leader: Go in peace, faith, and humility to love and serve the Good Shepherd who laid down his life for his sheep.
People: Thanks be to God.

A Holy Saturday Liturgy of the Labyrinth

THE OPENING

The congregation gathers by the labyrinth and stands or sits in prayer and quiet contemplation until signaled by the leader:

Together: I believe in the sun even when it is not shining,
I believe in love even when I cannot feel it,
I believe in God even when he is silent.[1]

Silence is kept for a moment. The leader and people then begin with this reading from Deuteronomy 5:6–18

Leader: I, Adonai, am your God who brought you out of the land of Egypt, the house of bondage: You shall have no other gods beside me.

People: Lead us in your way, O Lord, and write your law in our hearts

Leader: You shall not make for yourself a sculptured image, any likeness of what is in the heavens above, or on the earth below, or in the waters below the earth. You shall not bow down to them or serve them. For I your God Adonai am an impassioned God, visiting the guilt of the parents upon the children, upon the third and upon the fourth generations of those who reject me,

---

1. written on a prison cell wall at Auschwitz during the holocaust

A Holy Saturday Liturgy of the Labyrinth

People: but showing kindness to the thousandth generation of those who love me and keep my commandments.
Lead us in your way, O Lord, and write your law in our hearts

Leader: You shall not swear falsely by the name of your God Adonai; for Adonai will not clear one who swears falsely by God's name.
People: Lead us in your way, O Lord, and write your law in our hearts

Leader: Observe the sabbath day and keep it holy, as your God Adonai has commanded you. Six days you shall labor and do all your work, but the seventh day is a sabbath of your God Adonai; you shall not do any work—you, your son or your daughter, your male or female slave, your ox or your ass, or any of your cattle, or the stranger in your settlements, so that your male and female slave may rest as you do. Remember that you were a slave in the land of Egypt and your God Adonai freed you from there with a mighty hand and an outstretched arm; therefore your God Adonai has commanded you to observe the sabbath day.
People: Lead us in your way, O Lord, and write your law in our hearts

Leader: Honor your father and your mother, as your God Adonai has commanded you, that you may long endure, and that you may fare well, in the land that your God Adonai is assigning to you.
People: Lead us in your way, O Lord, and write your law in our hearts

Leader: You shall not murder.
People: Lead us in your way, O Lord, and write your law in our hearts

Leader: You shall not commit adultery.
People: Lead us in your way, O Lord, and write your law in our hearts

Leader: You shall not steal.
People: Lead us in your way, O Lord, and write your law in our hearts

Leader: You shall not bear false witness against your neighbor.
People: Lead us in your way, O Lord, and write your law in our hearts

Leader: You shall not covet your neighbor's wife. Likewise, none of you shall crave your neighbor's house, or field, or male or female slave, or ox, or ass, or anything that is your neighbor's.
People: Your way is love, O God. Lead us in your way, and write your law in our hearts.

THE LABYRINTH

The people now begin the labyrinth in whatever way is most practical for the space. As they progress, they should be encouraged to quietly repeat:

> Your way is love, O God. Lead us in your way, and write your law in our hearts.

If there is a reason why the people could not repeat their phrase, as the first person begins the labyrinth, the leader begins reading 1 Peter 3: 13–22:

> Now who will harm you if you are eager to do what is good? But even if you do suffer for doing what is right, you are blessed. Do not fear what they fear, and do not be intimidated, but in your hearts sanctify Christ as Lord. Always be ready to make your defense to anyone

who demands from you an accounting for the hope that is in you, yet do it with gentleness and respect. Maintain a good conscience so that, when you are maligned, those who abuse you for your good conduct in Christ may be put to shame. For it is better to suffer for doing good, if suffering should be God's will, than to suffer for doing evil. For Christ also suffered for sins once for all, the righteous for the unrighteous, in order to bring you to God. He was put to death in the flesh but made alive in the spirit, in which also he went and made a proclamation to the spirits in prison, who in former times did not obey, when God waited patiently in the days of Noah, during the building of the ark, in which a few, that is, eight lives, were saved through water. And baptism, which this prefigured, now saves you—not as a removal of dirt from the body but as an appeal to God for a good conscience, through the resurrection of Jesus Christ, who has gone into heaven and is at the right hand of God, with angels, authorities, and powers made subject to him.

Together: Our Father, who art in heaven,
    hallowed be thy Name,
    thy kingdom come,
    thy will be done,
        on earth as it is in heaven.
Give us this day our daily bread.
And forgive us our trespasses,
    as we forgive those who trespass against us.
And lead us not into temptation,
    but deliver us from evil.
For thine is the kingdom, and the power, and the glory,
    for ever and ever. Amen.

Holy Week and Easter

OPTIONAL COMMUNION

Here may be added a celebration of the Holy Eucharist.

THE PROCESSION INTO THE WORLD

Leader: The Lord be with you.
People: And with thy spirit.
Leader: Let us pray.

Leader: O God, who led the people of Israel out of Egypt and provided the law to set them free, write your law of love in our hearts. Help us through the winding desert paths of our lives, such that we find your way of love mapped out in our hearts. Remind us that through death upon the cross Jesus overcame death and led us to life. As Christ proclaimed salvation even to those who had died, let us hear the good news while still alive and receive your blessings of life eternal.

Leader: Go in peace, hope, and joy to love and serve the Lord.
People: Thanks be to God.

Easter

Easter is the summation of our church year: the day when death and sin are overcome by the power and love of God. It is a day and a season of perfect hope, but also a reminder of the need for repentance and humility.

Figure 7. Resurrection at Trinity Wall Street, inspired by Piero della Francesca. © Rob Elsner

An Easter Liturgy of the Labyrinth

If desired and possible in the space, the colors white or gold are preferred for decorations, banners, ribbons, etc.

THE OPENING

The congregation gathers by the labyrinth and stands or sits in prayer and quiet contemplation. The leader and people begin with these statements:

Leader: Why look for the living among the dead? Alleluia, he is risen!

People: He is risen indeed! Alleluia! Thanks be to God.

Leader: O Lord, whose death upon the cross was not the end, but the beginning of a new day and age for us all, grant us the ability to fully praise you and come into relation with you that our hearts may be filled and overflow with your love, praising you with our hearts, our minds, and our lives. Help us to overcome our fear of death and the grave, so that we see life everlasting through you. May our time together be focused on you in true worship and lead us to that holy country where with all the saints we may only see you.

Easter

THE LABYRINTH

The people now begin the labyrinth in whatever way is most practical for the space. As they progress through the labyrinth, the congregation should be encouraged to quietly repeat:

> You loved us enough to die for us, and loved us even more, so overcame death and lived for us. Your way is love, O God. Lead us in your way, and write your law in our hearts.

OPTIONAL COMMUNION

Here may be added a celebration of the Holy Eucharist.

THE PROCESSION INTO THE WORLD

Leader   The Lord be with you.
People   And also with you.
Leader: Let us pray.

Together: Our Father, who art in heaven,
> hallowed be thy Name,
> thy kingdom come,
> thy will be done,
>> on earth as it is in heaven.
>
> Give us this day our daily bread.
> And forgive us our trespasses,
>> as we forgive those who trespass against us.
>
> And lead us not into temptation,
>> but deliver us from evil.
>
> For thine is the kingdom, and the power, and the glory,
>> for ever and ever. Amen.

Leader: Let your hearts be light and filled with joy. Let the remembrance of Christ's birth, life, death, resurrection,

An Easter Liturgy of the Labyrinth

and ascension fill you with hope. May the Risen Lord be with us throughout this and every day. May we focus our faith and build relationships in his name. And may the peace of the Lord be with you now and forever. *Amen.*

Leader: Alleluia, he is risen! Go in peace, hope, and joy to love and serve the Lord.

People: He is risen indeed! Thanks be to God. Alleluia! Alleluia!

Between Easter and Trinity Sunday

Figure 8. Ascension at Trinity, Abbeville, SC, inspired by da Vinci. © Rob Elsner

An Ascension Day Liturgy of the Labyrinth

If desired and possible in the space, the color white is preferred for decorations, banners, ribbons, etc.

THE OPENING

Leader: Look up! He arises through the skies!
People: Yet the Holy Spirit remains with us! Thanks be to God.

The leader or a reader from the congregation then reads Christ's Commission to his disciples:

> Later Jesus appeared to the Eleven as they were eating; he rebuked them for their lack of faith and their stubborn refusal to believe those who had seen him after he had risen. He said to them, "Go into all the world and preach the gospel to all creation. Whoever believes and is baptized will be saved, but whoever does not believe will be condemned. And these signs will accompany those who believe: In my name they will drive out demons; they will speak in new tongues; they will pick up snakes with their hands; and when they drink deadly poison, it will not hurt them at all;

they will place their hands on sick people, and they will get well." After the Lord Jesus had spoken to them, he was taken up into heaven and he sat at the right hand of God. Then the disciples went out and preached everywhere, and the Lord worked with them and confirmed his word by the signs that accompanied it. *(Mark 16:14–20)*

THE LABYRINTH

The people now begin the labyrinth in whatever way is most practical for the space. As they progress through the labyrinth, the congregation should be encouraged to pray with words about the ascension and the presence of the Holy Spirit. A repeated pray might look like this:

> Look down from heaven, O Lord, and hear us when we call upon you.

OPTIONAL COMMUNION

Here may be added a celebration of the Holy Eucharist.

THE PROCESSION INTO THE WORLD

Leader   The Lord be with you.
People   And also with you.
Leader: Let us pray.

Together: Our Father, who art in heaven,
             hallowed be thy Name,
             thy kingdom come,
             thy will be done,
                on earth as it is in heaven.

An Ascension Day Liturgy of the Labyrinth

Give us this day our daily bread.
And forgive us our trespasses,
    as we forgive those who trespass against us.
And lead us not into temptation,
    but deliver us from evil.
For thine is the kingdom, and the power, and the glory,
for ever and ever. Amen.

Leader: Alleluia, he is risen from the dead and risen to the skies. Paise be to you, Holy Spirit, who remains with us to guide, comfort, and bless. With all the saints above and below, may the Father bless you, may the Son strengthen you, and may the Spirit of Truth comfort you. Alleluia! Alleluia! *Amen.*

Leader: Alleluia, he is risen! Go in peace, hope, and joy to love and serve the Lord.

People: He is risen indeed! Thanks be to God. Alleluia! Alleluia!

A Pentecost Liturgy of the Labyrinth

If desired and possible in the space, the color red is preferred for decorations, banners, ribbons, etc.

THE OPENING

Leader: The people of Israel celebrated the harvest, and the Holy Spirit came down.
People: Like tongues of fire above their heads, the apostles preached.
Leader: Lead us into the world to preach the gospel.
People: Guide us in your way of love.

All present read Psalm 119:105–12 responsively:

Leader: Your word is a lamp for my feet,
People: a light on my path.
Leader: I have taken an oath and confirmed it,
People: that I will follow your righteous laws.
Leader: I have suffered much;
People: preserve my life, LORD, according to your word.
Leader: Accept, LORD, the willing praise of my mouth,
People: and teach me your laws.
Leader: Though I constantly take my life in my hands,
People: I will not forget your law.
Leader: The wicked have set a snare for me,

A Pentecost Liturgy of the Labyrinth

People:	but I have not strayed from your precepts.
Leader:	Your statutes are my heritage forever;
People:	they are the joy of my heart.
Leader:	My heart is set on keeping your decrees
People:	to the very end.

THE LABYRINTH

The people now begin the labyrinth in whatever way is most practical for the space. As they progress through the labyrinth, the congregation should be encouraged to pray with words about the presence of the Holy Spirit.

> Breathe new life into me, O God, and fill me with your Holy Spirit

OPTIONAL COMMUNION

Here may be added a celebration of the Holy Eucharist.

THE PROCESSION INTO THE WORLD

Leader	The Lord be with you.
People	And also with you.
Leader:	Let us pray.

Leader and People

> Our Father, who art in heaven,
>   hallowed be thy Name,
>   thy kingdom come,
>   thy will be done,
>   on earth as it is in heaven.
> Give us this day our daily bread.
> And forgive us our trespasses,

Between Easter and Trinity Sunday

        as we forgive those who trespass against us.
And lead us not into temptation,
        but deliver us from evil.
For thine is the kingdom, and the power, and the glory,
        for ever and ever. Amen.

Together: Holy Spirit, Great Comforter, ignite your holy fire in our hearts; strengthen our faith to share the gospel in our words, in our thoughts, and in our deeds, breathe in revival to your church so that we can understand real rejoicing, through Jesus Christ our Lord. *Amen.*

Leader: The Spirit is with us! Go in peace to love and serve the Lord.

People: Thanks be to God. Amen.

A Trinity Sunday Liturgy of the Labyrinth

The first Sunday after Pentecost, Trinity Sunday, celebrates the doctrine of the Trinity: the Father, the Son, and the Holy Spirit. Traditionally, colorings are to be white if decorating around the labyrinth.

THE OPENING

The service begins with all reciting the Nicene Creed together:

> We believe in one God,
>   the Father, the Almighty,
>   maker of heaven and earth,
>   of all that is, seen and unseen.
> We believe in one Lord, Jesus Christ,
>   the only Son of God,
>   eternally begotten of the Father,
>   God from God, Light from Light,
>   true God from true God,
>   begotten, not made,
>   of one Being with the Father.
>   Through him all things were made.
>   For us and for our salvation
>   he came down from heaven:
>   by the power of the Holy Spirit

Between Easter and Trinity Sunday

> he became incarnate from the Virgin Mary,
> and was made man.
> For our sake he was crucified under Pontius Pilate;
> he suffered death and was buried.
> On the third day he rose again
> in accordance with the Scriptures;
> he ascended into heaven
> and is seated at the right hand of the Father.
> He will come again in glory to judge the living and the dead,
> and his kingdom will have no end.
> We believe in the Holy Spirit, the Lord, the giver of life,
> who proceeds from the Father and the Son.
> With the Father and the Son he is worshiped and glorified.
> He has spoken through the prophets.
> We believe in one holy catholic and apostolic church.
> We acknowledge one baptism for the forgiveness of sins.
> We look for the resurrection of the dead,
> and the life of the world to come. Amen.

THE LABYRINTH

A foot washing is appropriate, possibly using the suggested form on pp. 132–34. The people now begin the labyrinth in whatever way is most practical for the space. If a prompt is needed for prayer, the following is suggested:

> God in three persons, make me one with your way of love.

OPTIONAL COMMUNION

Here may be added a celebration of the Holy Eucharist.

A Trinity Sunday Liturgy of the Labyrinth

THE PROCESSION INTO THE WORLD

Leader   The Lord be with you.
People   And also with you.
Leader: Let us pray.

Together: Our Father, who art in heaven,
    hallowed be thy Name,
    thy kingdom come,
    thy will be done,
        on earth as it is in heaven.
  Give us this day our daily bread.
  And forgive us our trespasses,
    as we forgive those who trespass against us.
  And lead us not into temptation,
    but deliver us from evil.
  For thine is the kingdom, and the power, and the glory,
    for ever and ever. Amen.

Leader: Let us pray.

Together: Holy Trinity, incomprehensible in form and fashion, overwhelming in grace, mercy, and love. We your people praise, worship, and bless you, even when we do not understand. We trust in you, O God. We ask for you presence, protection, and blessings until in that heavenly country we see you face to face and finally understand fully. *Amen.*

Leader   Go in peace to love and serve our Triune God. Go therefore and make disciples of all nations, baptizing them in the name of the Father and of the Son and of the Holy Spirit.

People   Thanks be to God, Father, Son, and Holy Spirit. Amen.

Special Labyrinth Liturgies

An All Saints Day Liturgy of the Labyrinth

On All Saints, we celebrate the lives of all who have faithfully gone before us into the church victorious. Traditionally, colorings are to be white if decorating around the labyrinth.

THE OPENING

The congregation gathers by the labyrinth and stands or sits in prayer and quiet contemplation.

Leader: O Lord, whose saints above and below show us how to follow in your way;
Response: We praise you and thank you.
Leader: O Lord Jesus, whose disciples entered into glory and who inspired countless to follow you in love;
Response: We praise you and thank you.
Leader: O Holy Spirit, who empowered the saints to follow in spite of threats to life itself;
Response: We praise you and thank you.
Leader: Holy Lord, let us become like those saints who fill your heavenly courts. Empower us to have a steadfast faith and willingness to share your word with all the world in thought, word, and deed. *Amen.*

Special Labyrinth Liturgies

The leader or a reader from among the congregation should then read the following Scripture:

> I saw another angel ascending from the rising of the sun, having the seal of the living God, and he called with a loud voice to the four angels who had been given power to damage earth and sea, saying, "Do not damage the earth or the sea or the trees, until we have marked the servants of our God with a seal on their foreheads." And I heard the number of those who were sealed, 144,000, sealed out of every tribe of the people of Israel. After this I looked, and there was a great multitude that no one could count, from every nation, from all tribes and peoples and languages, standing before the throne and before the Lamb, robed in white, with palm branches in their hands. They cried out in a loud voice, saying, "Salvation belongs to our God who is seated on the throne, and to the Lamb!" And all the angels stood around the throne and around the elders and the four living creatures, and they fell on their faces before the throne and worshiped God, singing, "Amen! Blessing and glory and wisdom and thanksgiving and honor and power and might be to our God forever and ever! Amen." Then one of the elders addressed me, saying, "Who are these, robed in white, and where have they come from?" I said to him, "Sir, you are the one that knows." Then he said to me, "These are they who have come out of the great ordeal; they have washed their robes and made them white in the blood of the Lamb.
>
> "For this reason they are before the throne of God, and worship him day and night within his temple, and the one who is seated on the throne will shelter them. 'They will hunger no more, and thirst no more; the sun will not strike them, nor any scorching heat'; for the Lamb at the center of the throne will be their shepherd, and 'he will guide them to springs of

An All Saints Day Liturgy of the Labyrinth

the water of life,' and 'God will wipe away every tear from their eyes.'" *(Revelation 7:2–4, 9–17)*

THE LABYRINTH

A foot washing is appropriate, possibly using the suggested form on pp. 132–34. The people now begin the labyrinth in whatever way is most practical for the space. A suggested refrain for the labyrinth is:

> Let me have the faith of the saints to believe fully in your word, O Lord.

OPTIONAL COMMUNION

Here may be added a celebration of the Holy Eucharist or Special Prayers.

THE PROCESSION INTO THE WORLD

Leader   The Lord be with you.
People   And also with you.
Leader: Let us pray.

Together: Our Father, who art in heaven,
        hallowed be thy Name,
        thy kingdom come,
        thy will be done,
            on earth as it is in heaven.
    Give us this day our daily bread.
    And forgive us our trespasses,
        as we forgive those who trespass against us.
    And lead us not into temptation,
        but deliver us from evil.
    For thine is the kingdom, and the power, and the glory,
        for ever and ever. Amen.

Special Labyrinth Liturgies

Leader: Blessed are the poor in spirit,
People: for theirs is the kingdom of heaven.
Leader: Blessed are those who mourn,
People: for they will be comforted.
Leader: Blessed are the meek,
People: for they will inherit the earth.
Leader: Blessed are those who hunger and thirst for righteousness,
People: for they will be filled.
Leader: Blessed are the merciful,
People: for they will receive mercy.
Leader: Blessed are the pure in heart,
People: for they will see God.
Leader: Blessed are the peacemakers,
People: for they will be called children of God.
Leader: Blessed are those who are persecuted for righteousness' sake,
People: for theirs is the kingdom of heaven.
Leader: Blessed are you when people revile you and persecute you and utter all kinds of evil against you falsely on my account.
People: Rejoice and be glad, for your reward is great in heaven, for in the same way they persecuted the prophets who were before you.

Leader: Go in peace to love and serve our Eternal King.
People: Thanks be to God.

A Christ the King Sunday Liturgy of the Labyrinth

Christ the King Sunday celebrates the complete authority of Christ as King and Lord of creation, and is the last Sunday before Advent. Traditionally, colorings are to be white if decorating around the labyrinth.

THE OPENING

The congregation gathers by the labyrinth and stands or sits in prayer and quiet contemplation.

Leader: O Lord God, King of the Universe, who created and rules everything;
Response: We praise you and acknowledge you to be our King.
Leader: O Lord Jesus, King above all kings, through your death and resurrection you demonstrated that all powers and dominions, even that of death itself, are subject to you;
Response: We praise you and acknowledge you to be our King.
Leader: O Holy Spirit, whose loving kindness presides over our hearts;
Response: We praise you and acknowledge you to be our King.
Leader: Holy, Triune, indivisible God, you are King of kings and Lord of lords, free us from the bonds of sin.

Special Labyrinth Liturgies

Restore in us clean hearts, and show your mercy in our lives and the lives of all, both those we love and those whom we think we hate. Bless our enemies as much as our friends that we may all come to live under your reign and in your eternal kingdom for ever and ever. Amen.

THE LABYRINTH

A foot washing is appropriate, possibly using the suggested form on pp. 132–34. The people now begin the labyrinth in whatever way is most practical for the space. Suggested repeated prayer is:

> We praise you and acknowledge you to be our King

OPTIONAL COMMUNION

Here may be added a celebration of the Holy Eucharist or special prayers:

THE PROCESSION INTO THE WORLD

Leader   The Lord be with you.
People   And also with you.
Leader: Let us pray.

Together: Our Father, who art in heaven,
　　　　　　hallowed be thy Name,
　　　　　　thy kingdom come,
　　　　　　thy will be done,
　　　　　　　　on earth as it is in heaven.
　　　　Give us this day our daily bread.
　　　　And forgive us our trespasses,
　　　　　　as we forgive those who trespass against us.

A Christ the King Sunday Liturgy of the Labyrinth

> And lead us not into temptation,
> > but deliver us from evil.
> For thine is the kingdom, and the power, and the glory,
> > for ever and ever. Amen.

Leader: Let us pray.

Together: King Eternal, King Supreme, to whom all knees should bend, all heads bow. We praise you for all you have done, and ask your blessings on our lives. May we be good and faithful subjects and citizens of your eternal kingdom, where with all the saints we may come to rest and worship you forever. *Amen.*

Leader: Go in peace to love and serve our Eternal King.
People: Thanks be to God.

Figure 9. Washing of Feet at Georgetown, inspired by Albrecht Durer. © Rob Elsner

A Suggested Liturgy for the Washing of Feet

When appropriate and desired, this form may be used in a ceremony of foot washing.

Before the service begins, a pitcher of water and a bowl of some sort should be prepared, along with towels sufficient for each person. If more than two or three people's feet are to be washed, it is recommended that a large bucket be provided for waste water, and additional pitchers or bucket for fresh, clean water be readied. At least one chair, bench, or pew should be set up as the foot washing station. If the foot washing takes place indoors, it is highly advised that a plastic sheet be placed on the floor to prevent water damage to floors or dangerous slippery places upon which people might slip. Unless there is an ordained person present and administering, oil should not be used for blessing of the feet.

Leader: A reading from the Gospel according to John in the thirteenth chapter, verses 1–17:
It was just before the Passover Festival. Jesus knew that the hour had come for him to leave this world and go to the Father. Having loved his own who were in the world, he loved them to the end. The evening meal was in progress, and the devil had already prompted Judas, the son of Simon Iscariot, to betray Jesus. Jesus knew

that the Father had put all things under his power, and that he had come from God and was returning to God; so he got up from the meal, took off his outer clothing, and wrapped a towel around his waist. After that, he poured water into a basin and began to wash his disciples' feet, drying them with the towel that was wrapped around him. He came to Simon Peter, who said to him, "Lord, are you going to wash my feet?"

Jesus replied, "You do not realize now what I am doing, but later you will understand." "No," said Peter, "you shall never wash my feet." Jesus answered, "Unless I wash you, you have no part with me." "Then, Lord," Simon Peter replied, "not just my feet but my hands and my head as well!" Jesus answered, "Those who have had a bath need only to wash their feet; their whole body is clean. And you are clean, though not every one of you." For he knew who was going to betray him, and that was why he said not every one was clean.

When he had finished washing their feet, he put on his clothes and returned to his place. "Do you understand what I have done for you?" he asked them. "You call me 'Teacher' and 'Lord,' and rightly so, for that is what I am. Now that I, your Lord and Teacher, have washed your feet, you also should wash one another's feet. I have set you an example that you should do as I have done for you.

"Very truly I tell you, no servant is greater than his master, nor is a messenger greater than the one who sent him. Now that you know these things, you will be blessed if you do them."

The leader then pours water over each person's feet into the bowl one foot at a time, or begins with the first person who then washes the next person's feet. After pouring water, each foot should be patted dry with an individual towel.

A Suggested Liturgy for the Washing of Feet

Leader: After washing their feet, Jesus said to the disciples: "A new command I give you: Love one another. As I have loved you, so you must love one another. By this everyone will know that you are my disciples, if you love one another."

Chartres Labyrinth
RJFE 2023

Other Feast Day Liturgies

A Liturgy of the Labyrinth for St. Stephen's Day

December 26

Stephen was one of the first deacons of the church and the first martyr to the cause of Christ. He had led a life of service and compassion. Traditionally, colorings are to be red if decorating around the labyrinth.

THE OPENING

The congregation gathers by the labyrinth and stands or sits in prayer and quiet contemplation.

Reader: Now Stephen, a man full of God's grace and power, performed great wonders and signs among the people. Opposition arose, however, from members of the Synagogue of the Freedmen (as it was called)—Jews of Cyrene and Alexandria as well as the provinces of Cilicia and Asia—who began to argue with Stephen. But they could not stand up against the wisdom the Spirit gave him as he spoke. *(Acts 6:8–10)*

When the members of the Sanhedrin heard this, they were furious and gnashed their teeth at him. But Stephen, full of the Holy Spirit, looked up to heaven and saw the glory of God, and Jesus standing at the right hand of God. "Look," he said, "I see heaven open and the Son of Man standing at the right hand of God." At this they covered their ears and, yelling at the top of their voices, they all rushed at him, dragged him out of the city and began to stone him. Meanwhile, the witnesses laid their coats at the feet of a young man named Saul. While they were stoning him, Stephen prayed, "Lord Jesus, receive my spirit." Then he fell on his knees and cried out, "Lord, do not hold this sin against them." When he had said this, he fell asleep. (Acts 7:54–60)

Together: Jesus, our salvation and strength, we thank you for the example of Stephen, the first martyr of the faith. You gave him wisdom and a heart to serve other people. You strengthened him so that instead of cursing those who killed him, he prayed for their forgiveness. From his example many other hearts were turned to you and your love. Breathe into all here present your strength and wisdom, O Lord, and fill our hearts with such love that we can serve those in need and truly forgive those who hurt us in any way. *Amen.*

THE LABYRINTH

Begin the labyrinth in whatever way is most practical for the space, and if possible, sing or listen to the hymn "For All the Saints" or similar thematically appropriate music. At the center of the labyrinth, focus on trust in God and on forgiveness. Perhaps with a concluding statement such as:

A Liturgy of the Labyrinth for St. Stephen's Day December 26

Lord Jesus, receive my spirit. Lord, do not hold their sins against those who hurt me.

OPTIONAL COMMUNION

Here may be added a celebration of the Holy Eucharist or Special Prayers.

PROCESSION FROM LABYRINTH INTO THE WORLD

Leader: Give us strength to stand up for you, dear Lord.
People: Protect us from all who oppose your will.
Leader: God, who received the soul of Stephen and gave him a crown of glory, let us follow his example and serve whomever in need that we are able. Help us to be honestly forgiving and strong enough to not bear grudges. Let us see our own faults, fix them, and not compare ourselves to others except to learn to love you more. Amen.

A Feast of the Holy Innocents Liturgy of the Labyrinth

December 28

The Holy Innocents are considered martyrs, not because of their faith, but because of the focus on fear and hatred of Christ that King Herod had. Herod ordered the death of all baby boys so that Jesus could not take Herod's throne. Traditionally, colorings are to be red if decorating around the labyrinth.

THE OPENING

Sitting or standing, take a moment of quiet contemplation and then read the following scripture and pray:

Reader: Then Herod, when he saw that he was deceived by the wise men, was exceedingly angry; and he sent forth and put to death all the male children who were in Bethlehem and in all its districts, from two years old and under, according to the time which he had determined from the wise men. Then was fulfilled what was spoken by Jeremiah the prophet, saying:

"A voice was heard in Ramah,

A Feast of the Holy Innocents Liturgy of the Labyrinth December 28

> Lamentation, weeping, and great mourning,
> Rachel weeping for her children,
> Refusing to be comforted,
> Because they are no more." *(Matthew 2:16–18)*

Leader: Lord, we praise you for your creation, your mercy, and your love. Help us to comprehend that which we do not, especially the loss of life of innocent children. Deliver their souls to your eternal kingdom where they may never know pain or sorrow. Take away the hatred, arrogance, and desperation for control that promotes such evil in this world. Comfort those who have lost children under any circumstances, and let them accept such comfort such that they see your love and mercy in the circumstances and do not become embittered against you and your church. Help us cherish those with us, and remember all the great works you have done. Cause us to grow in faith every day, dear Lord.

THE LABYRINTH

Begin the labyrinth in whatever way is most practical for the space, and if desirable, sing or listen to the hymn "What Wondrous Love Is This" or "Jesus Loves the Little Children" or similar thematically appropriate music. At the center of the labyrinth, focus on seeking God's love in all things, even tragedies.

> Lord, I do not understand, but I trust you. Help me to see your plan and any the evil of humankind that opposes your will.

OPTIONAL COMMUNION

Here may be added a celebration of the Holy Eucharist or Special Prayers.

Other Feast Day Liturgies

PROCESSION FROM LABYRINTH
INTO THE WORLD

Together: Great Architect of the Universe, who set the universe in motion and created us to glorify you, I praise you for my life and the lives of those whom I love. Help me and all others to understand the deaths of the innocent, especially children. Whatever the circumstances, enlighten my mind and my heart to your will, your plans, and where we may have erred and strayed from your ways such that events like the massacre of the Holy Innocents transpire. Embolden me, O Lord, to make whatever changes I can to save life and avoid pain in others, so that all people can come to praise you in wholeness of heart. *Amen.*

A Feast of St. Joseph Liturgy of the Labyrinth

March 19

Joseph married Mary, even though pregnant by the overshadowing of the Holy Spirit. He protected Mary and Jesus through an honorable life. Traditionally, colorings are to be white if decorating around the labyrinth.

THE OPENING

Sitting or standing, take a moment of quiet contemplation and then pray after reading the following scripture:

Reader: Now the birth of Jesus Christ was on this wise: When as his mother Mary was espoused to Joseph, before they came together, she was found with child of the Holy Ghost. Then Joseph her husband, being a just man, and not willing to make her a public example, was minded to put her away privily. But while he thought on these things, behold, the angel of the Lord appeared unto him in a dream, saying, Joseph, thou son of David, fear not to take unto thee Mary thy wife: for that which is conceived in her is of the Holy Ghost. *(Matthew 1:18–20)*

Together: We thank you God, for the kindness and righteousness of Joseph, that he went against his societal conventions to become an earthly father to our Lord and Savior and a husband to Mary. Help us all to be slow to judge, and to listen to you and your angels present in our lives. Let us see truth and be considerate of others, now and always.

THE LABYRINTH

Begin the labyrinth in whatever way is most practical for the space, and if possible, sing or listen to the hymn "Lord of All Hopefulness" or similar thematically appropriate music. At the center of the labyrinth, focus on standing up for others, even when it brings inconvenience or ridicule to you.

> Strengthen me to be like Joseph, even at the cost of my comfort. Let me stand for what is right.

OPTIONAL COMMUNION

Here may be added a celebration of the Holy Eucharist or Special Prayers.

PROCESSION FROM LABYRINTH INTO THE WORLD

Together: Lord of all hopefulness, Lord of all joy, thank you for the life and ministry of Joseph. Help us all to be so bold and faithful to take on responsibilities that may terrify us, but which serve your plans for building your kingdom. Armor us with gentleness and kindness, and give us contentedness that peace is in our hearts. Amen.

A Feast of Mary Magdalene Liturgy of the Labyrinth

July 22

Mary Magdalene, named because she came from the city of Magdala, travelled with Jesus all over the land during his earthly ministry. She was the first person to see the Risen Lord and proclaim his resurrection to the other disciples. She served out of pure love, not only from gratitude at Jesus curing her of her burden of demons. She was one of the few who remained with Jesus, even at the cross and at the grave.

THE OPENING

Sitting or standing, take a moment of quiet contemplation and then pray:

Leader: When Jesus rose early on the first day of the week, he appeared first to Mary Magdalene, out of whom he had driven seven demons. *(Mark 16:9)*

Together: Lord, thank you for the life and example of Mary of Magdala, the first to proclaim Jesus as having risen from the dead. As Mary put all of her trust in Jesus and ministered to him and to the apostles, teach me

Other Feast Day Liturgies

to trust in you and to minister to your people as they need. Prepare my heart, O God, to let your love flow through me and bless those around me. Let me not be dismayed, Lord, but overwhelm the world with your mercy.

THE LABYRINTH

Begin the labyrinth in whatever way is most practical for the space, and if possible, sing or listen to the hymn "Take My Life and Let It Be" or similar thematically appropriate music. At the center of the labyrinth, focus on

> Lord, let me be a servant of truth and mercy. Give me strength for healing others, always trusting in you so that I too am healed.

OPTIONAL COMMUNION

Here may be added a celebration of the Holy Eucharist or Special Prayers.

PROCESSION FROM LABYRINTH INTO THE WORLD

Together: Savior, Redeemer, and Friend, you comforted Mary and she comforted you and your disciples. Comfort me and help me to comfort other people. Stay with me in all times, as Mary stayed with Jesus at the cross. Open our ears that we may only hear truth about other people, and not utter falsehoods. Open our eyes to see where we might help others and support them. Strengthen our bodies that we might serve others in whatever ways that truly glorifies you. Give us patience such that we see your plans in your time. *Amen.*

A Feast of St. Mary the Virgin Liturgy of the Labyrinth

August 15

Mary took upon herself the responsibility to become the Mother of God. She knew she would face difficulties and that her child's life would be filled with tragedy as well as joy, but she did what was right for the salvation of the world. Traditionally, colorings are to be white if decorating around the labyrinth.

THE OPENING

Sitting or standing, take a moment of quiet contemplation, read the following scripture and then pray:

Reader: And in the sixth month the angel Gabriel was sent from God unto a city of Galilee, named Nazareth, to a virgin espoused to a man whose name was Joseph, of the house of David; and the virgin's name was Mary. And the angel came in unto her, and said, Hail, thou that art highly favoured, the Lord is with thee: blessed art thou among women. And when she saw him, she was troubled at his saying, and cast in her mind what manner of salutation this should be. And the angel said unto her,

Fear not, Mary: for thou hast found favour with God. And, behold, thou shalt conceive in thy womb, and bring forth a son, and shalt call his name JESUS. He shall be great, and shall be called the Son of the Highest: and the Lord God shall give unto him the throne of his father David: And he shall reign over the house of Jacob for ever; and of his kingdom there shall be no end. Then said Mary unto the angel, How shall this be, seeing I know not a man? And the angel answered and said unto her, The Holy Ghost shall come upon thee, and the power of the Highest shall overshadow thee: therefore also that holy thing which shall be born of thee shall be called the Son of God. *(Luke 1:26–35)*

Together: We thank you, dearest Lord, for the life and faith of Mary. Although young, she followed her faith in spite of societal pressures that she knew would condemn her. She risked all for you and your plan of salvation for the world. Grant us such strength of conviction and such awareness of the world that we may not be bitter at the load you give us to bear. Strengthen us for service, Lord, and grant us the resolve to carry through all our tasks of love. *Amen.*

THE LABYRINTH

Begin the labyrinth in whatever way is most practical for the space, and if possible, sing or listen to the hymn "Blest Are the Pure in Heart" or "Ave Maria" or "Salve Regina" or similar thematically appropriate music. A suggested prayer for the journey is:

Take my life, Lord, to fulfill your purposes. Bind me with faith and love, and never let me falter.

OPTIONAL COMMUNION

Here may be added a celebration of the Holy Eucharist or Special Prayers.

PROCESSION FROM LABYRINTH INTO THE WORLD

Reader: And Mary said, My soul doth magnify the Lord, and my spirit hath rejoiced in God my Saviour. For he hath regarded the low estate of his handmaiden: for, behold, from henceforth all generations shall call me blessed. For he that is mighty hath done to me great things; and holy is his name. And his mercy is on them that fear him from generation to generation. He hath shewed strength with his arm; he hath scattered the proud in the imagination of their hearts. He hath put down the mighty from their seats, and exalted them of low degree. He hath filled the hungry with good things; and the rich he hath sent empty away. He hath holpen his servant Israel, in remembrance of his mercy; As he spake to our fathers, to Abraham, and to his seed for ever. And Mary abode with her about three months, and returned to her own house. *(Luke 1:46–51)*

Together: We praise you, Ruler of Heaven, for the life and example of Mary, Mother of God. Through her strength of faith she was able to bear and raise our Lord, caring for him and ministering to him in his times of need. Help all of your children to have the faith and resolve of Mary, that we too may follow and serve. Take away our fears and doubts, even if you do not send angels that we recognize to reassure us. *Amen.*

A Feast of St. Michael and All Angels Liturgy of the Labyrinth

September 29

Traditionally, colorings are to be white if decorating around the labyrinth.

THE OPENING

Sitting or standing, take a moment of quiet contemplation, read Psalm 103:19–22, and then pray. (Please consider using the asterisks below/above for pauses or indicators of change if responsively reading by half verse.)

Together: The Lord has set his throne in heaven, *
 and his kingship has dominion over all.
Bless the Lord, you angels of his, you mighty ones who do his bidding, *
 and hearken to the voice of his word.
Bless the Lord, all you his hosts, *
 you ministers of his who do his will.
Bless the Lord, all you works of his, in all places of his dominion; *
 bless the Lord, O my soul.

A Feast of St. Michael and All Angels Liturgy of the Labyrinth September 29

Leader: Everlasting God, who created all things, thank you for the angels who minister to us all, whether we perceive their presence or not. As angels ministered to Jesus in the wilderness and also brought to our forebearers messages of peace and of warning, please send your angels to minister to our fears and doubts that we might fully honor you with our lives. We praise you for Michael and other angels who we know do battle against the forces of evil, and we ask to be strengthened to combat all sin that separates us from you. *Amen.*

THE LABYRINTH

Begin the labyrinth in whatever way is most practical for the space, and if possible, sing or listen to the hymn "Holy God We Praise Thy Name" or similar thematically appropriate music. At the center of the labyrinth, focus on the messages for which angels are known. A prayer to repeat might be:

> Open my mind, Lord, to hear the messages you send. Grant your angels protect me.

OPTIONAL COMMUNION

Here may be added a celebration of the Holy Eucharist or Special Prayers.

PROCESSION FROM LABYRINTH INTO THE WORLD

Reader: I saw the LORD seated on a throne, high and exalted; and the train of his robe filled the temple. Above him stood seraphim, each having six wings: With two wings they covered their faces, with two they covered

Other Feast Day Liturgies

their feet, and with two they were flying. And they were calling out to one another:
"Holy, holy, holy is the Lord of Hosts;
all the earth is full of his glory."
At the sound of their voices the doorposts and thresholds shook, and the temple was filled with smoke. *(Isaiah 6:1–4)*

Together: Glory to you, Creator of all things, Judge of all people, who made angels to be messengers to humanity. Angels spoke with Jacob and Abraham, with Joshua and with the disciples. Angels worship you day and night, while we should be doing the same. We thank you for the angels and the reminders of your love and protection which aid and assist in saving us so often from ourselves and our lack of faith. As the Archangel Michael leads the heavenly host in battle against evil, so empower each of us to fight off the snares and traps of evil in all its forms here on earth. Help us be angels of mercy and kindness here on earth, spreading the good news of salvation and hope to all people. *Amen.*

A Feast of St. James of Jerusalem Liturgy of the Labyrinth

October 23

James was a martyr for the church. He was the first Bishop of Jerusalem and helped ensure that all people were welcomed into the church. Traditionally, colorings are to be red if decorating around the labyrinth.

THE OPENING

Sitting or standing, take a moment of quiet contemplation, read this passage from the Epistle of James, and then pray:

Reader: Wherefore, my beloved brethren, let every man be swift to hear, slow to speak, slow to wrath: For the wrath of man worketh not the righteousness of God. Wherefore lay apart all filthiness and superfluity of naughtiness, and receive with meekness the engrafted word, which is able to save your souls. But be ye doers of the word, and not hearers only, deceiving your own selves. For if any be a hearer of the word, and not a doer, he is like unto a man beholding his natural face in a glass: For he beholdeth himself, and goeth his way, and straightway forgetteth what manner of man he was. But whoso looketh into the perfect law of liberty, and continueth therein, he being not a forgetful hearer, but a doer of the work, this man shall be blessed in his deed. If any man among you seem to be religious, and bridleth not his tongue, but deceiveth his own heart, this man's religion is vain. Pure religion and undefiled before God and the Father is this, To visit the fatherless and widows in their affliction, and to keep himself unspotted from the world. *(James 1:19–27)*

Together: Lord, thank you for the work of James, first Bishop of Jerusalem. His life and teachings help us grow to be honest and good, truly doers of the word, not just hearers. Help us to hear and do your word and commandments in our lives and share into the lives of others that we may all know you and serve you with all of our hearts and minds and strength. Guard our tongues so that the words we speak may be sweet and pure, always to your glory and the benefit to all your creation. *Amen.*

THE LABYRINTH

Begin the labyrinth in whatever way is most practical for the space, and if possible, sing or listen to the hymn "By All Your Saints Still Striving" or similar thematically appropriate music. At the center of the labyrinth, focus on doing, not just hearing the gospel. An appropriate repeating prayer might be:

> Help me to do the works you have given me, O God, not simply hearing them. Write your laws in my heart and make my actions true.

OPTIONAL COMMUNION

Here may be added a celebration of the Holy Eucharist or Special Prayers.

PROCESSION FROM LABYRINTH INTO THE WORLD

Reader: Who is wise and understanding among you? Let him show it by his good conduct, by deeds done in the humility that comes from wisdom. But if you harbor bitter jealousy and selfish ambition in your hearts, do not boast in it or deny the truth. Such wisdom does not come from above, but is earthly, unspiritual, demonic. For where jealousy and selfish ambition exist, there will be disorder and every evil practice. But the wisdom from above is first of all pure, then peace-loving, gentle, accommodating, full of mercy and good fruit, impartial, and sincere. Peacemakers who sow in peace reap the fruit of righteousness. *(James 3:13–18)*

Together: Thank you, Lord, for the life and work of the apostle James. Help us to do all you have given us to do and to be humble and honest throughout our lives and interactions with each other. Give us pure hearts that can honestly be content and yet willing to work for your purposes. Guide us to avoid evil and arrogance, and stand for truth, even in spite of risks. *Amen.*

Special Occasion Labyrinth Liturgies

A Liturgy of Healing in the Labyrinth

THE OPENING

The congregation gathers by the labyrinth and stands or sits in prayer and quiet contemplation. If the weather or conditions permit, each person should be encouraged to make an ablution (hand washing) in a small basin.

Leader: O Lord God, King of the Universe, who set the stars and planets in their courses;
Response: We praise you and bless your creation.
Leader: O Holy Spirit, who moved over the face of the waters and caused life to begin;
Response: We praise you and bless your creation.
Leader: O Father of us all, who formed us from clay and breathed life into us;
Response: We praise you and bless your creation.
Leader: O Jesus, who caused the blind to see, the lame to walk, and the dead to be restored;
Response: We praise you and bless your creation.
Leader: Holy God, Lover of souls, we ask for healing in mind, body, and soul;
Response: We praise you and bless your creation.
Leader: Look upon all your children, O God;
Response: Who put their trust in you.
Leader: Lay your healing hand upon us;

Special Occasion Labyrinth Liturgies

Response: Say the word and we shall be healed.

Leader: Lord, our paths are not straight and wide, but curved and narrow. Guide us to you and your healing presence, dearest Lord. Let us feel your grace and power in healing. Let us no longer be bent over in pain, but stand and praise God.

THE LABYRINTH

A foot washing is appropriate, possibly using the suggested form on pp. 132–34. The people now begin the labyrinth in whatever way is most practical for the space. A journey prayer would be something like:

Heal me, Lord, and heal all those in need.

At the center of the labyrinth, the minister should stand or sit and lay hands on each person as they arrive at the center, saying:

Leader: Adonai Rafa, Great Physician, you have shown miracles of healing throughout time. Bless this your beloved child. Heal *her/him* of pain, suffering, and confusion. Strengthen *her/him* for your service in faith and focus. We ask this in the Name of the Father, Son, and Holy Spirit. Amen.

When each person has completed the journey, they should stand or be seated in silent prayer until all are finished. The labyrinth courses may be followed in silence or in singing of a chant, such as "Ubi Caritas" as appropriate to the traditions of the congregation.

OPTIONAL COMMUNION

Here may be added a celebration of the Holy Eucharist or Special Prayers.

A Liturgy of Healing in the Labyrinth

THE PROCESSION INTO THE WORLD

Leader The Lord be with you.
People And also with you.
Leader: Let us pray.

Together: Our Father, who art in heaven,
   hallowed be thy Name,
   thy kingdom come,
   thy will be done,
      on earth as it is in heaven.
Give us this day our daily bread.
And forgive us our trespasses,
   as we forgive those who trespass against us.
And lead us not into temptation,
   but deliver us from evil.
For thine is the kingdom, and the power, and the glory,
   for ever and ever. Amen.

Leader: Let us pray.

Together: Almighty and loving God, who knows all the hairs on our heads and all stars in the heavens, we thank you for the centering of our hearts and minds on you, your mercy, and your love for us. We beg your mercy that our path may be simple and wide, with no stumbling blocks before us. Heal our brokenness where we are afflicted in mind, body, or spirit. Pour out your love and healing upon us now and always. Have mercy on us, beloved Lord, through Jesus Christ, with you and the Holy Ghost, be all honor and glory, world without end. *Amen.*

Leader: The peace of God, which passes all understanding, keep our hearts and minds in the knowledge and love of God, and mercy and compassion of Jesus Christ,

Special Occasion Labyrinth Liturgies

and the guidance and fellowship of the Holy Spirit. The blessing of God Almighty, the Father, the Son, and the Holy Ghost, be amongst us, and remain with us always. *Amen.*

Leader: Go in peace to love and serve the Lord.
People: Thanks be to God.

A Wedding/Anniversary Liturgy in the Labyrinth

This liturgy is not to supplant the traditional wedding service, but used alongside it and for anniversaries. Traditionally, colorings are to be white if decorating around the labyrinth.

THE OPENING

This liturgy may be used immediately after a wedding or in the days and weeks that follow, including as an anniversary rededication of the vows. Sitting or standing, take a moment of quiet contemplation and then begin:

Leader: The bond and covenant of marriage was established by God in creation, and our Lord Jesus Christ adorned this manner of life by his presence and first miracle at a wedding in Cana of Galilee. It signifies to us the mystery of the union between Christ and his church, and Holy Scripture commends it to be honored among all people.
People: Your way is love, O Lord, keep us in your way.
Leader: All life is relationship, and you caused us to be so that we may love you;
People: Let your love inform us so that our love might guide us to peace.

Special Occasion Labyrinth Liturgies

Leader: Jesus, you sacrificed your life that we may live;
People: In our faith in you, let us love each other as you love us.
Leader: O Holy Spirit, the promised Comforter of all;
People: Teach us how to comfort one another and guide us to love you more.

Leader: Let us who have gathered in this place celebrate the union of these two people in heart and mind and body. Let us invoke the blessings of heaven that they may face all obstacles together. Let us commit ourselves to supporting them through all times of good and bad, sickness and health, dispute and agreement.

THE LABYRINTH

A foot washing is appropriate, possibly using the suggested form on pp. 132–34. The people now begin the labyrinth in whatever way is most practical for the space. The couple should journey through the labyrinth holding hands if possible, stopping at each turn and saying a private prayer together, such as "We turn together on our path to you, O God," or repeating "Love one another as Christ loved us." At the center of the labyrinth, the leader should stand or sit and encircle the hands of the married couple, saying:

Leader: Look mercifully upon these your children, O Lord, and assist them with your grace, that with true fidelity and steadfast love they may honor and keep the promises and vows they made to each other and to you. We beg your blessings of wisdom and patience that they may strengthen each other and be good companions, comforting and counseling one another, binding their loves ever more closely to you. Help them to be ever more faithful to your image, showing mercy and compassion, forgiveness and fulfillment. Make their love pure and focused on each other, save only the love they focus even more on you, Creator, Redeemer, and

A Wedding/Anniversary Liturgy in the Labyrinth

Sustainer of the world. We ask all of this through Jesus Christ our Savior, who lives and reigns with you in the unity of the Holy Spirit, one God, for ever and ever. Amen.

Couple: Lord of all hopefulness, deserving of all praise, we pledge our love to you and to one another. Grant us peace and strength to show each other kindness and mercy. Help us to strengthen our faith in you that all of our problems may not be stumbling blocks, but challenges we face together that strengthen our marriage. Make us always love each other as you love us, now and always. Amen.

When each person has completed the journey, they should stand or be seated in silent prayer until all are finished. The labyrinth courses may be followed in silence or in singing of a chant, such as "Ubi Caritas" as appropriate to the traditions of the congregation.

OPTIONAL COMMUNION

Here may be added a celebration of the Holy Eucharist or Special Prayers.

THE PROCESSION FROM LABYRINTH INTO THE WORLD

Together: Our Father, who art in heaven,
    hallowed be thy Name,
    thy kingdom come,
    thy will be done,
        on earth as it is in heaven.
Give us this day our daily bread.
And forgive us our trespasses,
    as we forgive those who trespass against us.
And lead us not into temptation,

Special Occasion Labyrinth Liturgies

> but deliver us from evil.
> For thine is the kingdom, and the power, and the glory,
> for ever and ever. Amen.

Leader: Have mercy on us, O God, according to your steadfast love; according to your abundant mercy blot out our transgressions. Wash us thoroughly from our iniquity, and cleanse us from our sin[1] Bless this marriage of two souls, Beloved Lord, that your way of love is evident in all they do. Have mercy on us, beloved Lord, through Jesus Christ, who with you and the Holy Ghost, be all honor and glory, world without end. Amen.

---

1. Psalm 51:1–2 ESV

A Liturgy of Reconciliation in the Labyrinth

While there is no ecclesiastical/liturgical tradition for this, suggested colorings are to be white if decorating around the labyrinth.

THE OPENING

Sitting or standing, take a moment of quiet contemplation and then pray:

Leader: O God, who has blessed us with rational minds and loving hearts, help us to focus on you. As children of Adam and Eve, we know that we are fallen. We beg you, O God, to forgive us so that we may be reconciled to other people and to you. Fill our hearts with your peace. Remind us always of the words Christ taught us: Forgive us our trespasses as we forgive those who trespass against us. For if we do not forgive one another, neither will you forgive us. Let us always submit to your will, walk in your ways, and love other people as you love us: in holiness, peace, and forgiveness. Help us to reconcile with those with whom we are out of good and wholesome relationship. Help us to reconcile with others so that we might participate in the communion of souls that is our faith.

Special Occasion Labyrinth Liturgies

Leader: Out of the depths I cry to you, Lord;
People: Lord, hear my voice.
Leader: Let your ears be attentive
People: to my cry for mercy.
Leader: If you, Lord, kept a record of sins,
People: Lord, who could stand?
Leader: But with you there is forgiveness,
People: so that we can, with reverence, serve you.
Leader: I wait for the Lord, my whole being waits,
People: and in his word I put my hope.
Leader: I wait for the Lord
People: more than watchmen wait for the morning,
Leader: Israel, put your hope in the Lord,
People: for with the Lord is unfailing love and with him is full redemption.
Leader: He himself will redeem Israel
People: from all their sins. *(Psalm 130)*

Leader: Lord Jesus, your blessed cross is a symbol of our brokenness and sin. We ask your guidance and peace that we may be reconciled to you, to all those with whom we have had problems or offended, and to all your creation. Let each of us present take up the cross and follow you as Simon of Cyrene did, helping you to complete your purposes on this earth. Like Simon, we are strangers to your kingdom. Like Simon, we can only carry the cross for a short time, and know that we do not suffer the crucifixion that redeemed us. Let us suffer for you only to learn to release all that we carry to your final care that our lives may truly be dedicated to you in love.

Palms or wooden crosses should be carried through the labyrinth.

A Liturgy of Reconciliation in the Labyrinth

THE LABYRINTH

A foot washing is appropriate, possibly using the suggested form on pp. 132–34. The people now begin the labyrinth in whatever way is most practical for the space. If possible, all should sing along, or have a soloist perform the hymn "Amazing Grace" or similar thematically appropriate music. A basket of palm or wooden/paper crosses should be provided. Crosses can then be handed out to the people present, each taking a cross to carry through the labyrinth. At the center of the labyrinth, the minister should stand or sit and lay hands on each person as they arrive at the center, saying:

Leader: In the name of our Blessed Redeemer, I ask you to put down that cross. Let the burden of contention cease. Be at peace and love one another as Christ loves us. Let us learn to love ourselves so that there is no room in our hearts for disagreement or arrogance.

Each places the cross in the center of the labyrinth. The labyrinth courses may be followed in silence or in singing of a chant, such as "Ubi Caritas" as appropriate to the traditions of the congregation. When all have completed the labyrinth, the leader continues:

Leader: Mark's Gospel tells us that "they compelled a passerby, Simon of Cyrene, who was coming in from the country, the father of Alexander and Rufus, to carry [Christ's] cross." Help us, O Lord, to carry your cross when you ask, and to understand why we are compelled with the burden. Help us, God, to know that we are not you and are not the ones crucified for our own sins. *Amen*

OPTIONAL COMMUNION

Here may be added a celebration of the Holy Eucharist or the following:

Leader: Heal us, Lord

Special Occasion Labyrinth Liturgies

People: Bind us together as your people
Leader: Hold us, Lord
People: Bind us together as your people
Leader: Teach us, Lord
People: Bind us together as your people

THE PROCESSION INTO THE WORLD

Leader   The Lord be with you.
People   And also with you.
Leader: Let us pray.

Together: Our Father, who art in heaven,
    hallowed be thy Name,
    thy kingdom come,
    thy will be done,
        on earth as it is in heaven.
Give us this day our daily bread.
And forgive us our trespasses,
    as we forgive those who trespass against us.
And lead us not into temptation,
    but deliver us from evil.
For thine is the kingdom, and the power, and the glory,
    for ever and ever. Amen.

Leader: Let us pray.

Together: O God, you made us in your own image and redeemed us through Jesus your Son: look with compassion on the whole human family; take away the arrogance and hatred that infect our hearts; break down the walls that separate us; unite us in bonds of love; and work through our struggle and confusion to accomplish your purposes on earth; that, in your good time, all nations and races may serve you in harmony around your heavenly throne; through Jesus Christ our Lord. *Amen.*

A Liturgy of Reconciliation in the Labyrinth

Leader: Forgive us, God, for what we have done and left undone, for sins unknown and that burden our hearts. Tear down all walls that separate us or cause us to be defensive or arrogant, so that we may serve you in wholeness of being. The peace of God, which passes all understanding, keep our hearts and minds in the knowledge and love of God, and mercy and compassion of Jesus Christ, and the guidance and fellowship of the Holy Spirit. The blessing of God Almighty, the Father, the Son, and the Holy Ghost, be amongst us, and remain with us always. *Amen.*

Leader: Go in peace, unity, and forgiveness to love and serve the Lord.
People Thanks be to God.

A Labyrinth Liturgy for Liberation

Liberation can be freedom from many issues and evils that bind us. Traditionally, colorings are to be white if decorating around the labyrinth.

THE OPENING

Sitting or standing, take a moment of quiet contemplation and then pray, beginning with this reading from Luke's Gospel:

Reader: He went to Nazareth, where he had been brought up, and on the Sabbath day he went into the synagogue, as was his custom. He stood up to read, and the scroll of the prophet Isaiah was handed to him. Unrolling it, he found the place where it is written:
"The Spirit of the Lord is on me,
because he has anointed me
to proclaim good news to the poor.
He has sent me to proclaim freedom for the prisoners
and recovery of sight for the blind,
to set the oppressed free,
to proclaim the year of the Lord's favor."
Then he rolled up the scroll, gave it back to the attendant and sat down. The eyes of everyone in the

A Labyrinth Liturgy for Liberation

synagogue were fastened on him. He began by saying to them, "Today this scripture is fulfilled in your hearing." *(Luke 4:16–21)*

Leader: O Author of Freedom, by whose might and mercy we are free, look on your creation with compassion. Help us to remember all who are not free, in body, mind, or spirit. Break the chains of oppression of all types, especially those that we cannot understand. Empower us to love and serve you and all of your people. Awaken our eyes to see your mercy and truth in all things, all situations, and all people. Give us patience, O Lord, but also give us the strength to work for your purposes, freeing ourselves and others where we are not free. Remind us each day that you are the source of all freedom. "It is for freedom that Christ has set us free. Stand firm, then, and do not let yourselves be burdened again by a yoke of slavery." *(Galatians 5:1)*

THE LABYRINTH

Begin the labyrinth in whatever way is most practical for the space, and if possible sing or listen to a hymn or similar thematically appropriate music. At the center of the labyrinth, focus on what freedom means to you, for yourself and for others. If you cannot find words to pray, repeat something like this:

> Lord, help me understand what freedom is, giving myself to you and to you alone. Help me to act where I can to free others, that they may find and love you.

OPTIONAL COMMUNION

Here may be added a celebration of the Holy Eucharist or Special Prayers.

Special Occasion Labyrinth Liturgies

PROCESSION FROM LABYRINTH INTO THE WORLD

Leader: Now the Lord is the Spirit, and where the Spirit of the Lord is, there is freedom. *(2 Corinthians 3:17).*

Together: Lord, pour into us knowledge and understanding of freedom. Help us to see freedom as more than simply not wearing chains or the ability to move around. Remind each of us, Lord, that there are forms of freedom we may not understand, and types of slavery we cannot know. Empower us, Beloved God, to act as agents and instruments of freedom, helping deliver others from their bonds where we can. Give us sympathy and empathy for others, freeing us from arrogance, embracing us further with your love. *Amen.*

A Labyrinth Liturgy for Justice

There are many forms of justice, and all come from God. Beyond traditions, it is suggested colorings are to be purple if decorating around the labyrinth.

THE OPENING

Sitting or standing, take a moment of quiet contemplation and then pray:

Reader: Seek the LORD and live,
 lest he break out like fire in the house of Joseph,
  and it devour, with none to quench it for Bethel,
 O you who turn justice to wormwood
  and cast down righteousness to the earth!
 But let justice roll down like waters
  and righteousness like an ever-flowing stream.
 (Amos 5:6–7, 24)

Together: Cloak me in a love of justice, O God, and empower me to stand up for those who cannot stand up for themselves. Let all forms of justice wash over me and clean me from all selfishness, jealousy, or ill intent that may taint my soul. Let my thirst for justice be true, selfless, and to your glory.

Special Occasion Labyrinth Liturgies

Reader: And he told them a parable to the effect that they ought always to pray and not lose heart. He said, "In a certain city there was a judge who neither feared God nor respected man. And there was a widow in that city who kept coming to him and saying, 'Give me justice against my adversary.' For a while he refused, but afterward he said to himself, 'Though I neither fear God nor respect man, yet because this widow keeps bothering me, I will give her justice, so that she will not beat me down by her continual coming.'" And the Lord said, "Hear what the unrighteous judge says. And will not God give justice to his elect, who cry to him day and night? Will he delay long over them? I tell you, he will give justice to them speedily. Nevertheless, when the Son of Man comes, will he find faith on earth?" (Luke 18:1–8)

Together: Build my faith, O God. Help me to believe and trust in you more and more each day.

A palm, stone, or wooden/paper cross could be carried by each person through the labyrinth as a reminder of the burden of justice. If you carry such a burden, leave it at the center of the labyrinth.

THE LABYRINTH

Begin the labyrinth in whatever way is most practical for the space, and if possible, sing or listen to the hymn or similar thematically appropriate music. At the center of the labyrinth, focus on being truly just and equitable to all people, honoring God's commands to us all. Alternately, read and reread the following scripture to help you pray:

> Thus says the LORD: Do justice and righteousness, and deliver from the hand of the oppressor him who has been robbed. And do no wrong or violence to the resident alien, the fatherless, and the widow, nor shed innocent blood in this place. *(Jeremiah 22:3)*

OPTIONAL COMMUNION

Here may be added a celebration of the Holy Eucharist or Special Prayers.

PROCESSION FROM LABYRINTH INTO THE WORLD

Together: Our Father, who art in heaven,
    hallowed be thy Name,
    thy kingdom come,
    thy will be done,
        on earth as it is in heaven.
Give us this day our daily bread.
And forgive us our trespasses,
    as we forgive those who trespass against us.
And lead us not into temptation,
    but deliver us from evil.
For thine is the kingdom, and the power, and the glory,
    for ever and ever. Amen.

Together: Judge Supreme, who is the final authority on all things, cleanse our hearts and minds of any inclination to be unjust, bitter, or vindictive. Let your divine justice ring from every tower, and fly as banners for us to see. Declare us innocent of all evil and hatred so that we might become pure. In your great wisdom and compassion, make us serve your kingdom and build that city of peace where all your children are loved and injustice cannot enter. *Amen.*

A Mother's Day Liturgy for the Labyrinth

Mother's Day celebrates the love and dedication of mothers and mothering people, and is celebrated the second Sunday of May. Traditionally, colorings are to be white if decorating around the labyrinth.

THE OPENING

Sitting or standing, take a moment of quiet contemplation and then pray:

Leader: Your mother was like a vine in a vineyard planted beside the waters; she bore lush fruit and foliage because of the plentiful water, and she produced mighty branches, fit for rulers' scepters. *(Ezekiel 19:10–11)*

When a woman gives birth, she has pain because her time has come. But when the child is born, she no longer remembers her distress because of her joy that a child has been born into the world. *(John 16:21)*

Jerusalem, Jerusalem, you who kill the prophets and stone those sent to you, how often I have longed to gather your children together, as a hen gathers her chicks under her wings, and you were not willing.

A Mother's Day Liturgy for the Labyrinth

Look, your house is left to you desolate. *(Matthew 23:37–38)*

Together: O Lord God, who protects us like a mother hen and cares for our every need, I think you for those who have mothered to me. Help me to cherish the mothers in my life and in the lives around me.

THE LABYRINTH

Begin the labyrinth in whatever way is most practical for the space. At the center of the labyrinth, or during the whole journey, consider repeating:

O God who bore us and gave us life, bless all mothers and those who act as mothers to us, your children. Amen.

PROCESSION FROM LABYRINTH INTO THE WORLD

Together: O God, author of life. You are parent and sibling to us. Look with compassion on all mothers. Strengthen those who struggle with any parts or facets of mothering. Gladden the hearts of mothers that they may cause other hearts to be eternally loving and hopeful. Heal those who wanted to be mothers but could not for whatever reason. Guide those who are mothering such that their children flourish. *Amen.*

Special Public Holiday Liturgies of the Labyrinth

A Labyrinth Liturgy for Dr. Martin Luther King, Jr. Day

The life, ministry, and civil rights actions of Dr. Martin Luther King, Jr. are celebrated the third Monday in January. Traditionally, colorings are to be red if decorating around the labyrinth.

THE OPENING

Sitting or standing, take a moment of quiet contemplation and then pray:

Leader: King of Heaven, by whose eternal and faithful love we were all created in your image, help us to see you in all our fellow travelers through this life. Thank you, our only Master, for the life and work of Dr. Martin Luther King, Jr. and all others who have worked and struggled and gave their lives for the cause of freedom. Help me to feel and honor the sacrifice of all those whose names are lost to history who struggled for the full justice of equality and dignity.

People: O God, you made us in your own image and redeemed us through Jesus your Son: look with compassion on the whole human family; take away the arrogance and hatred that infect our hearts; break down the walls that separate us; unite us in bonds of love; and work through our struggle and confusion to accomplish your purposes on earth; that, in your good time, all nations and races may serve you in harmony around your heavenly throne; through Jesus Christ our Lord. Amen.[1]

THE LABYRINTH

Begin the labyrinth in whatever way is most practical for the space, and if possible, sing or listen to the hymn "There Is a Balm in Gilead," "Rock of Ages," or similar thematically appropriate music. During the labyrinth journey, consider a repeated prayer such as:

> The sacrifices of God are a broken spirit: a broken and a contrite heart, O God, thou will not despise. *(Psalm 51:17)*
>
> Give me strength to love and forgive. Remove from me all thirst for vengeance, replaced by a hunger for forgiveness and peace. Let me love beyond measure and seek justice and unity beyond hope.

At the center of the labyrinth, try not to focus on when you have felt oppressed or belittled, but rather focus on the times in your life where you have felt that you may have oppressed, belittled, or dismissed the personhood of another child of God, asking God for forgiveness and remembering God's loving mercy.

OPTIONAL COMMUNION

Here may be added a celebration of the Holy Eucharist or Special Prayers.

---

1. BCP, 815

A Labyrinth Liturgy for Dr. Martin Luther King, Jr. Day

PROCESSION FROM LABYRINTH INTO THE WORLD

Together: Creator of all, in whose image we are all made from the same clay and dust, we thank you for the life and example of Dr. Martin Luther King, Jr. and all others who have fought the good fight for unity, peace, and equality. Grant that in our hearts we may grow to love all your creation, and show dignity and respect to all people, especially those with whom I disagree or towards whom I have hard feelings. Help me to stand up for justice, even when it is uncomfortable and has risk. Let us see from the mountaintop the wonders of your beloved world and strive to build your kingdom. *Amen.*

A Labyrinth Liturgy for Independence Day

July 4

Independence Day celebrates the founding of the United States as an independent nation after its revolution from England. Traditionally, colorings are to be red, white, or green if decorating around the labyrinth, depending on how the occasion is celebrated.

THE OPENING

Sitting or standing, take a moment of quiet contemplation and then pray:

Reader: You have heard that it was said, "You shall love your neighbor and hate your enemy." But I say to you, Love your enemies and pray for those who persecute you, so that you may be children of your Father in heaven; for he makes his sun rise on the evil and on the good, and sends rain on the righteous and on the unrighteous. For if you love those who love you, what reward do you have? Do not even the tax collectors do the same? And if you greet only your brothers and sisters, what more are you doing than others? Do not even the Gentiles do the same? Be perfect, therefore, as your heavenly Father is perfect. *(Matthew 5:43–48)*

Leader: Almighty Ruler of Heaven and Earth, by whose grace this country was founded on the bases of life, liberty, and the pursuit of happiness, we praise you for this land. Continue to us your blessings of prosperity and the willingness to share with those in need. Guide us all, we beseech you, to continue to bless this nation and guide us to maintain the concepts of freedom and welcome that have built a strong nation. Teach us continued and increasing justice, compassion, and peace. Bless all who strive for the ideals of this nation, ideals that focus on you and the liberty to worship you. Amen.

THE LABYRINTH

Begin the labyrinth in whatever way is most practical for the space, and if possible, sing or listen to a patriotic hymn from the hymnal or similar thematically appropriate music. In the labyrinth, focus on praying or repeating phrases like:

> Guide us to love and serve you, that this country resembles your kingdom. Thank you for those who have struggled for justice and peace.

OPTIONAL COMMUNION

Here may be added a celebration of the Holy Eucharist or Special Prayers.

Special Public Holiday Liturgies of the Labyrinth

PROCESSION FROM LABYRINTH INTO THE WORLD

Reader: For the L ORD your God is God of gods and Lord of lords, the great God, mighty and awesome, who is not partial and takes no bribe, who executes justice for the orphan and the widow, and who loves the strangers, providing them food and clothing. As You shall fear the L ORD your God; him alone you shall worship; to him you shall hold fast, and by his name you shall swear. He is your praise; he is your God, who has done for you these great and awesome things that your own eyes have seen. *(Deuteronomy 10:17–21)*

Together: Great King of Heaven and Earth, whose service is perfect freedom, liberate our hearts and minds that we might serve you and this nation. Strengthen our faith so that we can be more compassionate and be a true peacemaker, especially with those we perceive to be our enemies. Empower us to be humble and true to you and to this land that we may fulfill our potential of blessing all the peoples of the world. In your Holy Name we pray. *Amen.*

A Labyrinth Liturgy for Columbus/Indigenous People's Day

Columbus Day and Indigenous People's Day are celebrations of the relationships of peoples of the world and a day to remember that those relationships are not always good and respectful. It is a day of humility and thanksgiving on the second Monday in October. This holiday goes beyond church tradition, so colorings should be white if decorating around the labyrinth.

THE OPENING

Sitting or standing, take a moment of quiet contemplation and then pray:

Together: Great Chief who rules all the tribes of heaven and earth, we celebrate this day of remembrance. For some, this day is a celebration of discovery and opening of new realms and resources. For others, it is a day of mourning for the loss of sovereignty and peace. Unite us under the banner of your kingdom, that peace and kindness prevail, and that every proud division cease so that we form into one nation under your divine love. Let us sing your praises with many voices in our many languages, each praising you in a special and needed way. Bind us together, Sovereign King of the

Special Public Holiday Liturgies of the Labyrinth

Universe, so that we are all your chosen people and all remember that we are loved by you.

THE LABYRINTH

Begin the labyrinth in whatever way is most practical for the space, and if possible, sing or listen to the hymn or similar thematically appropriate music. Consider a repeated prayer such as:

> Give me courage to seek new places for your worship, O God. Open my heart to all people, Lord. Take away my fear, arrogance, and pride so that your love conquers all.

OPTIONAL COMMUNION

Here may be added a celebration of the Holy Eucharist or Special Prayers.

PROCESSION FROM LABYRINTH INTO THE WORLD

Together: Let us give thanks to you, loving God, and praise your name in this free land. Empower us to aid the cause of justice. Embolden us to honor all traditions of the peoples who make this place their home. Write your laws in our hearts, and in the hearts of all people, that we truly form into one country of love, welcoming the presence of your kingdom, where across ever shining seas and fertile lands your Name will be praised, and fear and hunger are but a memory. *Amen.*

A Liturgy of the Labyrinth for Thanksgiving Day

Thanksgiving Day celebrates the bounty of the earth and the sharing with those less fortunate. It occurs on the fourth Thursday in November. Traditionally, colorings are to be green if decorating around the labyrinth.

THE OPENING

Sitting or standing, take a moment of quiet contemplation and then read Psalm 100 and pray together. (Please consider using the asterisks below/above for pauses or indicators of change if responsively reading by half verse.)

Leader: Be joyful in the Lord, all you lands; *
serve the Lord with gladness and come before his presence with a song.
Know this: The Lord himself is God; *
he himself has made us, and we are his; we are his people and the sheep of his pasture.
Enter his gates with thanksgiving; go into his courts with praise; *
give thanks to him and call upon his Name.
For the Lord is good; his mercy is everlasting; *
and his faithfulness endures from age to age.

Special Public Holiday Liturgies of the Labyrinth

Together: Rejoice, starry heavens, crystal seas, and fruitful earth, for the Lord has made you. Rejoice all people of the earth, for the Lord has made you and has shown great love for you. God has promised plenty to those who trust in him, and this land has been blessed richly. Thank you, Lord of all, for what you have given us. Guide our minds to clearly see all is from your bounty and not of our own merit. Let us revel in your blessings, even when they seem scarce. Let us remember that this early life is short, and we need to be quick to bless others so that they also give thanks to you and praise your name. *Amen.*

THE LABYRINTH

Begin the labyrinth in whatever way is most practical for the space, and if possible, sing or listen to the hymn or similar thematically appropriate music. Consider a repeated prayer such as:

> Thank you, Heavenly Ruler, for all that I have. Help me to see the riches you shower upon me.

OPTIONAL COMMUNION

Here may be added a celebration of the Holy Eucharist or Special Prayers.

PROCESSION FROM LABYRINTH INTO THE WORLD

Leader: When they found him on the other side of the sea, they said to him, "Rabbi, when did you come here?" Jesus answered them, "Very truly, I tell you, you are looking for me, not because you saw signs, but because you ate your fill of the loaves. Do not work for the food that perishes, but for the food that endures for eternal life, which the Son of Man will give you. For it is on him that God the Father has set his seal." Then they said to him, "What must we do to perform the works of God?" Jesus answered them, "This is the work of God, that you believe in him whom he has sent." So they said to him, "What sign are you going to give us then, so that we may see it and believe you? What work are you performing? Our ancestors ate the manna in the wilderness; as it is written, 'He gave them bread from heaven to eat.'" Then Jesus said to them, "Very truly, I tell you, it was not Moses who gave you the bread from heaven, but it is my Father who gives you the true bread from heaven. For the bread of God is that which comes down from heaven and gives life to the world." They said to him, "Sir, give us this bread always." Jesus said to them, "I am the bread of life. Whoever comes to me will never be hungry, and whoever believes in me will never be thirsty. (*John 6:25–35*)

Together: Thank you, Founder of All Feasts, for the many blessings we have received from your hands. Remind us always that all comes from your grace, not the sweat of our brows. Enlighten our hearts to remember those less fortunate, so that we can be blessings to them in your name. Fill us with love and kindness that we may truly reflect your image. *Amen.*

A Labyrinth Liturgy for President's Day

President's Day celebrates those individuals who have tried to lead their country to the best of their ability. It is celebrated on the third Monday in February. Traditionally, colorings are to be green if decorating around the labyrinth.

THE OPENING

Sitting or standing, take a moment of quiet contemplation and then pray:

Reader: Where there is no guidance, a people falls, but in an abundance of counselors there is safety. *(Proverbs 11:14)*

With upright heart he shepherded them and guided them with his skillful hand. *(Psalm 78:72)*

"It shall not be so among you. But whoever would be great among you must be your servant, and whoever would be first among you must be your slave, even as the Son of Man came not to be served but to serve, and to give his life as a ransom for many." *(Matthew 20:26–28)*

A Labyrinth Liturgy for President's Day

Leader: O Lord our Governor, whose glory is in every country of the world; thank you for the life and leadership of all presidents and other leaders of this country. We beseech you to keep this nation in your merciful care. Inspire all who lead to continually be guided by your grace and blessings, that mercy and love define our land and that we may dwell secure in thy peace. Grant to the president of the United States, and to all in authority, wisdom and strength to know and to do your will. Fill our current leader and all future leaders with humility, honesty, integrity, and a love of truth and righteousness. Surround all leaders with the confidence of your love that they do not define their rule with fear, hatred, or persecution of your people, and remind them that you are the ultimate authority under whose kingship they preside. We pray this in the name of Jesus Christ our Lord, who lives and reigns with you and the Holy Spirit, one God, world without end. Amen.

THE LABYRINTH

Begin the labyrinth in whatever way is most practical for the space. At the center of the labyrinth, focus on what leadership means to this country and the world: Consider a repeated prayer such as:

> O Lord, guide and defend our rulers and mercifully hear us when we call upon thee.

OPTIONAL COMMUNION

Here may be added a celebration of the Holy Eucharist or Special Prayers.

Special Public Holiday Liturgies of the Labyrinth

PROCESSION FROM LABYRINTH INTO THE WORLD

Reader: For by the grace given to me I say to everyone among you not to think of himself more highly than he ought to think, but to think with sober judgment, each according to the measure of faith that God has assigned. For as in one body we have many members, and the members do not all have the same function, so we, though many, are one body in Christ, and individually members one of another. Having gifts that differ according to the grace given to us, let us use them: if prophecy, in proportion to our faith; if service, in our serving; the one who teaches, in his teaching; the one who exhorts, in his exhortation; the one who contributes, in generosity; the one who leads, with zeal; the one who does acts of mercy, with cheerfulness. *(Romans 12:3–8)*

Together: We thank you, O Lord, for all those called to political service in our nation, and especially for our president. We ask that they would all serve the people with integrity, truth, compassion, and justice. Grant wisdom, O Lord, that peace and harmony may prevail under their oversight, and that all citizens, guests, and visitors to our country may be respected as beloved children of God. *Amen.*

A Labyrinth Liturgy for Memorial Day

Memorial Day celebrates those who have given their lives in service of their country, or who served and have since died. It is celebrated on the last Monday of May. Traditionally, colorings are to be red if decorating around the labyrinth.

THE OPENING

Sitting or standing, take a moment of quiet contemplation and then pray:

Reader: This is my commandment, that you love one another as I have loved you. Greater love has no one than this, that someone lay down his life for his friends. You are my friends if you do what I command you. No longer do I call you servants, for the servant does not know what his master is doing; but I have called you friends, for all that I have heard from my Father I have made known to you. You did not choose me, but I chose you and appointed you that you should go and bear fruit and that your fruit should abide, so that whatever you ask the Father in my name, he may give it to you. These things I command you, so that you will love one another. *(John 15:12–17)*

Special Public Holiday Liturgies of the Labyrinth

Together: Commander of all the forces of heaven, who created and rules the universe. You have blessed the peacemakers. We praise you this day as we remember those who have given their lives in service to their country. Hold their souls in the palm of your hand, forgiving them of any sins and cherishing their selflessness and bravery to serve. You chose them, Lord, even if they did not choose you. Let light perpetual shine on them and those who loved them. Glory to you, Lord of all, who remembers those widowed and orphaned by wars and catastrophes, and gives them comfort. *Amen.*

THE LABYRINTH

Begin the labyrinth in whatever way is most practical for the space. At the center of the labyrinth, focus on remembering the sacrifices of those fallen in service to their country. Consider a repeated prayer such as:

> Blessed are the peacemakers and those who fought for causes they thought just. Give peace in our time.

OPTIONAL COMMUNION

Here may be added a celebration of the Holy Eucharist or Special Prayers.

PROCESSION FROM LABYRINTH
INTO THE WORLD

Reader: Blessed is the nation whose God is the Lord, the people whom he has chosen as his heritage! The Lord looks down from heaven; he sees all the children of man; from where he sits enthroned he looks out on all

A Labyrinth Liturgy for Memorial Day

the inhabitants of the earth, he who fashions the hearts of them all and observes all their deeds. The king is not saved by his great army; a warrior is not delivered by his great strength. The war horse is a false hope for salvation, and by its great might it cannot rescue. Behold, the eye of the Lord is on those who fear him, on those who hope in his steadfast love, that he may deliver their soul from death and keep them alive in famine. Our soul waits for the Lord; he is our help and our shield. For our heart is glad in him, because we trust in his holy Name. Let your steadfast love, O Lord, be upon us, even as we hope in you. (*Psalm 33:12–22*)

Together: Lord of all, by whose kindness peace is established. We, your children, have rebelled against you and brought war, corruption, and injustice to the earth. We praise you and thank you, Almighty God, for the lives of those women and men who have served their country and lain down their lives in defense of justice and freedom. Comfort those who have survived the loss of these defenders of freedom, and bless those now serving to have the strength and bravery to complete their tasks, and the wisdom to avoid death when possible. While we see that death is not the end, Lord, we know that it is a great fear among your people. Strengthen our faith more than our arms, O God, that our trust is always in you. *Amen.*

A Labyrinth Liturgy for Veteran's Day

November 11

Veteran's Day celebrates those who have served their country and are still living. Traditionally, colorings are to be green or white if decorating around the labyrinth.

THE OPENING

Sitting or standing, take a moment of quiet contemplation and then pray:

Reader: And he said, The Lord is my rock and my fortress and my deliverer; My God, my rock, in whom I take refuge; My shield and the horn of my salvation, my stronghold and my refuge; My savior, Thou dost save me from violence. I call upon the Lord, who is worthy to be praised; And I am saved from my enemies. (2 Samuel 22:2–4)

Together: Author of Life and Peace, we praise you and glorify your Name for having given women and men to serve in the armed forces of this nation to protect us all. Let us appreciate their sacrifices: those who serve and those whose service is complete. Help us to see that their work is and has been in the pursuit of peace and justice, empowering all to make the decisions to follow you and love you.

THE LABYRINTH

Begin the labyrinth in whatever way is most practical for the space, and if possible, sing or listen to the hymn "America the Beautiful," "God of Our Fathers," "Almighty Father, Strong to Save," or similar thematically appropriate music. At the center of the labyrinth, focus on those who have served their country and may have scars, visible and invisible. During the labyrinth journey, consider a repeated prayer such as:

For veterans:

> The LORD is my rock, my fortress and my deliverer; my God is my rock, in whom I take refuge, my shield and the horn of my salvation, my stronghold. *(Psalm 18:2)*

For those who are not veterans:

> For those who defend our country, I give thanks. For those who will sacrifice, I ask comfort.

OPTIONAL COMMUNION

Here may be added a celebration of the Holy Eucharist or Special Prayers.

Special Public Holiday Liturgies of the Labyrinth

PROCESSION FROM LABYRINTH INTO THE WORLD

Reader: We ought always to thank God for you, brothers and sisters, and rightly so, because your faith is growing more and more, and the love all of you have for one another is increasing. Therefore, among God's churches, we boast about your perseverance and faith in all the persecutions and trials you are enduring. *(2 Thessalonians 1:3–4)*

Together: Ruler of Heaven and Earth, whose angels have charge over us to bring us messages of truth. You have given us wisdom and rational minds to think through all things. Help us to honor those who serve to defend this country, that they might show wisdom, compassion, and mercy, making hard decisions concerning all your children. Let the strength of their hearts be even greater than the strength of their arms. Pour into them faith and integrity that they do not lose their way. Bind up and heal all wounds of body, mind, and soul that may trouble those who have served. Enfold us all in your love that we may see the end to all war and violence, joining hands to worship you throughout all ages. *Amen.*

Resources and References

Baldovin, John F. *Liturgy in Ancient Jerusalem*. Piscataway, NJ: Gorgias, 2010.
Candolini, G. *Labyrinths: Walking toward the Center*. New York: Crossroad, 2003.
Danaher, James P. *Contemplative Prayer: A Theology for the Twenty-First Century*. Eugene, OR: Cascade, 2011.
Episcopal Church. *The Book of Common Prayer and Administration of the Sacraments and Other Rites and Ceremonies of the Church: Together with the Psalter or Psalms of David: According to the use of the Episcopal Church*. New York: Church Hymnal Corp, 1979.
Fontana, David. *The Secret Language of Symbols: A Visual Key to Symbols and Their Meanings*. San Francisco: Chronicle, 2001.
Jacobs, O. "A Definition of Liturgy." *Orate Fratres* 9.11 (1935) 506–11.
Kavanagh, Aiden. *On Liturgical Theology*. Collegeville, MN: Liturgical, 1992.
Kavanaugh, Kiernan. "Contemplation and the Stream of Consciousness." In *Carmelite Prayer: A Tradition for the 21st Century*, edited by Keith J. Egan, 101–18. New York: Paulist, 2003.
Keating, Thomas. "Contemplative Prayer in Christian Tradition." In *Finding Grace at the Center*, edited by T. Keating, M. B. Pennington, and T. E. Clark, 35–47. 4th ed. Petersham, MA: St. Bede's, 1985.
Matthews W. H. *Mazes and Labyrinths: Their History and Development*. New York: Dover, 1970.
McLuhan, Marshall. *Understanding Media: The Extensions of Man*. New York: McGraw-Hill, 1964.
Miller, J. H. "The Nature and Definition of the Liturgy." *Theological Studies* 18.3 (1957) 325–56.
Neville, Gwen Kennedy, and John H. Westerhoff III. *Learning through Liturgy*. New York: Seabury, 1978.
O'Connor Elizabeth. *Search for Silence*. Rev. ed. San Diego: LuraMedia, 1986.
Pennington, M. Basil. *Centering Prayer: Renewing an Ancient Christian Prayer Form*. New York: Doubleday, 1982.

Resources and References

———. "Centering Prayer." In *Finding Grace at the Center*, edited by T. Keating, M. B. Pennington, and T. E. Clark, 3–31. 4th ed. Petersham, MA: St. Bede's. 1985.

Price, Charles P., and Louis Weil. *Liturgy for Living*. Harrisburg, PA: Morehouse, 2000.

Rule of Benedict. Prologue 1. https://ccel.org/ccel/benedict/rule/rule.ii.html

Ruth, Leicester, Carrie Steenwyk, and John D. Witvliet. *Walking Where Jesus Walked: Worship in Fourth-Century Jerusalem*. Grand Rapids: Eerdmans, 2010.

Van Olst, E. H. *The Bible and Liturgy*. Grand Rapids: Eerdmans, 1991.

Wallraff, Martin, Silvana Seidel Menchi, and Kaspar von Greyerz, eds. *Basel 1516: Erasmus' Edition of the New Testament*. Tübingen: Mohr Siebeck, 2016.

Welch, S. *Walking the Labyrinth: A Spiritual and Practical Guide*. Norwich, UK: Canterbury, 2010.

Wright, Craig .M. *The Maze and the Warrior: Symbols in Architecture, Theology, and Music*. Cambridge: Harvard University Press, 2001.

About the Author

Robert Elsner (PhD, DMin) is professor and chair of psychology at Samford University in Birmingham, Alabama, USA. Rob holds degrees from the University of North Carolina at Chapel Hill, École Le Cordon Bleu de Paris, the University of Georgia, University College Cork, Erskine Theological Seminary, and Virginia Theological Seminary. A gerontologist specializing in Alzheimer's disease, Rob has always been active in the church. At VTS, his work focused on empowering college students for evangelism. After seminary, he taught Christian education, homiletics, and other seminary courses over the years, and founded and directed the MA in counseling program at Erskine Theological Seminary. He and his wife, Betsy, met while studying in Paris at Le Cordon Bleu. Betsy is an academic librarian. They have two children. Rob has walked labyrinths since the 1960s and started taking them seriously in the 1980s, walking them throughout the US and Europe.

www.ingramcontent.com/pod-product-compliance
Lightning Source LLC
Chambersburg PA
CBHW062026220426
43662CB00010B/1495